Dating For Men Playbook

Powerful Dating Advice for Men - Including How to Effortlessly Attract Women and Boost Your Self-Esteem and Confidence – Plus, Tinder Secrets to Help You Master the Online Dating Game

Author: Christian Ford

Table Of Contents

Part 1: Preparing to Date 1

   Chapter 1: The Top 10 Things That Women Want in a Man 1

   Chapter 2: Being Confident in Who You Are and What You Have to Offer 8

   Chapter 3: Are You Ready to Date? 12

Part 2: Finding and Having Your First Date 15

   Chapter 4: Dating in the Modern World 15

   Chapter 5: Online Dating & Dating Apps 18

   Chapter 6: Where to Find a Potential Date 32

   Chapter 7: Your Approach 35

   Chapter 8: Planning the First Date 41

   Chapter 9: Getting Ready for Your Date 45

   Chapter 10: Making Conversation 53

   Chapter 11: Enjoying Your Date 57

   Chapter 12: Bad Dates 65

Part 3: The Second Date and Beyond 77

   Chapter 13: The Second Date 77

   Chapter 14: The Stages of Dating 88

   Chapter 15: Moving Forward...Slowly 94

   Chapter 16: Breaking Up 98

Introduction	107
Chapter One: The Principles of Self-Esteem	109
Chapter Two: Self-Acceptance; a Pathway to Cultivating High Self-Esteem	115
Chapter Three: How to Live Purposefully	119
Chapter Four: Getting Rid of Happiness Anxieties	126
Chapter Five: Being Conscious of Self	134
Chapter Six: Using the Mind as a Force Field	140
Chapter Seven: You are Enough!	147
Chapter Eight: Winning the War Within	153
Chapter Nine: Being Responsible Toward Reality	159
Chapter Ten: A Commitment to Learning Always	165
Chapter Eleven: Kicking Addictions Out	171
Chapter Twelve: How do you treat others?	178
Chapter Thirteen: Humility is a Tool	184
Chapter Fourteen: Falling in Love with Yourself	192
Chapter Fifteen: The Art of Sustaining Self-Esteem	199
Conclusion	207

Part 1: Preparing to Date

Chapter 1: The Top 10 Things That Women Want in a Man

Before jumping into how to find the girl of your dreams – or at least a first date – let's take a glance at what it takes to be the man of hers.

Obviously, every woman is different, and what one woman finds attractive in a man may not appeal to another. That being said, enough surveys and studies have been done in recent years to provide a pretty good understanding of what women generally look for in a man.

1. A Sense of Humor

Study after study has found that a sense of humor is the top characteristic that women find attractive in a man. Don't own a fancy car? Don't have six-pack abs? Those things really don't matter as much to most women as the ability to smile and have fun.

You don't have to be a professional comedian or the class clown to show you have a sense of humor. However, the ability to find humor in frustrating situations and laugh at yourself without being self-deprecating is very attractive to women. Having a good sense of humor also means that you laugh – or at least smile – when she says something humorous. Women love a man who smiles and who is not afraid of a heart-felt chuckle.

2. Self Confidence

The idea of dating can be intimidating; and if you aren't comfortable, it shows. The first thing to remember is that you are just looking for a date, not a life partner at this point. One date. If it goes badly, chalk it up as a learning experience and move on to the next one. Don't let your self confidence fade because you are putting too much pressure on one date.

When first meeting a woman, a lot of guys instantly lose any chance they might have had with her by coming off as insecure. It's okay to be a little nervous, and it's even okay to let your date know you're a little nervous. But don't let that insecurity take over.

The good news is that even if you feel nervous and insecure, there are ways to fake it. Maintain eye contact. Speak slowly, clearly, and directly. Use humor. Ask questions to keep the conversation flowing. Smile. Make decisions. Move slowly. All of these things deliver a calm, cool confidence that women find extremely attractive.

Let's back up and clarify that self confidence is not the same as cockiness. Confidence comes from seeing yourself in a realistic way, recognizing the strengths and assets that you bring to the table. (We will talk more about this in Chapter 2.) Cockiness is just bragging to show off, and often comes without the skills and knowledge to back it up. Knowing the difference allows you to feel good about yourself and what you can offer your date.

3. A Positive Attitude

Pessimists, complainers, whiners, "doom-and-gloom" theorists, worriers, critics, and so on. Sounds likes a fun date, right? It's no wonder women list having a positive attitude as an important attribute in a man.

People generally want to be around people who make them feel good; and happy people often make other people happy. Women and men alike prefer to be around people who make them feel better about themselves and their lives.

Dates are a great time to show off your positivity. Having to wait longer than anticipated for a table at dinner? Look at it as an opportunity to get to know each other. Traffic jam? Use the time to talk or to find out what kind of music your date likes. Meal less than ideal? Joke about it.

Staying positive in negative situations is a very attractive trait; and again, it's one you can learn with some practice. Start by stopping yourself when you catch yourself complaining or starting to say something negative. Additionally, practicing positivity can improve your self-confidence. By learning to be more positive, you will stop putting yourself down.

4. A Good Conversationalist

Women generally enjoy talking, and when looking for a potential partner they want someone who can carry on a conversation. Conversations require give and take, which means both listening and talking with your date.

Remember that being shy is OK. In fact, many women prefer a little bit of shyness compared to the super-loud alpha male type. The key is to not be so shy that you don't talk at all. Instead, ask questions and practice listening.

When it comes to conversations, sports and cars are okay in moderation, but women typically will want to be able to talk about "life stuff," especially as the relationship begins to grow. Sometimes these kinds of conversations can become overwhelming for guys, but if you can push through the discomfort and attempt to listen, it will do wonders in helping you develop a relationship.

If you aren't an expert on a topic, don't pretend you are. Instead, let her tell you what she knows about it. Pay attention and ask questions. If the topic is something you are well-versed in and passionate about, pay attention to her body language and make sure she's interested - and never be condescending.

5. Kind, Thoughtful, and Generous

Women like men who are kind and thoughtful - not just to them - but to everyone, including strangers. In dating, thoughtfulness includes small gestures that indicate you respect and appreciate your partner. It doesn't necessarily mean you have to buy her diamonds or send her flowers. Even small gestures like remembering what she likes on her pizza or suggesting you both watch her favorite TV show together can mean a lot to a woman.

In addition to treating your date well, women appreciate men who treat others kindly. Opening doors for strangers, treating waiters politely, or simply thanking the cashier at a store or drive-through all win brownie points with women.

Women also like men who are generous, whether it's tipping the waiter, dropping a coin in the Salvation Army's bucket, or donating time or money to charity.

6. Patience

Much like being kind and thoughtful, women like men who are patient. A man who is patient represents emotional maturity as well as empathy, both of which are very sexy traits to women. Barking at the customer service rep for being left on hold or blowing a gasket because you're caught in traffic is not attractive.

Patience, like positivity, is one of those things that can actually be learned and cultivated when intentionally practiced. One way is to try to imagine what your reaction to a situation looks like to the strangers around you. No woman is going to see you snapping your fingers at the waiter and think, "Wow, I wish I was with *him*!"

Another way to help you become more patient is to try to put the situation into perspective. Will your date be ruined if it takes 10 extra minutes to get your drinks? Probably not, but it could be ruined if you throw a fit because you didn't get your drinks sooner.

7. Honest and Trustworthy

It's no surprise that women cherish honesty. This extends well beyond simply being faithful in a relationship. It also includes clearing up expectations early on and throughout the relationship. (Maybe not on the first date though.)

While being up front about certain things can sometimes be challenging, especially if it's going to hurt the other person's feelings, it helps make the relationship smoother in the long run so that resentments aren't given the opportunity to simmer.

8. A Sense of Adventure

Before you go sign up for SCUBA lessons, you need to understand this one a little bit. A "sense of adventure" does not necessarily mean doing something big or dangerous. Not every woman wants a mountain climber or a sky diver. However, women do like men who are willing to try new things.

Whether it's trying out a new restaurant, venturing to watch the ballet, or simply getting out on the dance floor with her, being able to step out of your comfort zone will earn you huge bonus points as a date.

9. Emotionally Available and Present

Women are generally just naturally better at emotions than men. Women often want to know how you are feeling, which can be challenging - because you may not even know yourself. However, it's important to at least try to discuss how you are feeling, especially when she asks. Women particularly want to know when they've done something that has made you happy or sad.

10. Shared Values

With the rest of the characteristics that women are drawn to, there are things you can do to make yourself more attractive. This one, however, is a little tougher.

You and your date are not going to agree on everything, and that's OK. But there are some issues where different values may just not make for a great fit. For example, if one of you is a devout Christian and the other is an atheist, you may not be a good match. If one is a staunch vegan and the other is an avid hunter - again, there may be some differences that are too big to overcome.

What's Missing from This List?

Did you notice some things that were missing from this list? Let me give you a hint. There was nothing on it that had to do with how you look or how much money you make.

Yes, these things can make a difference in the very beginning, but most women tend to move past a man's looks and the size of his wallet if these other 10 characteristics are strong. And the best part is, with the exception of number 10, these are all attributes that can be developed and strengthened with practice.

Chapter 2: Being Confident in Who You Are and What You Have to Offer

As mentioned in Chapter 1, a key factor that women find attractive in a man is confidence.

We all struggle with things that we'd like to improve about ourselves. Our weight. Our height. Our smile. Our voice. Our job. Our checkbook. In our minds, our shortcomings can become overwhelming – like that's all anyone ever notices about us. It's scary, and it can be paralyzing. But the reality is that those things don't have to define us.

The key to being confident is not being the best looking or wealthiest guy in the room. It's electing not to be afraid. It's not letting the fear of rejection keep you from approaching a woman. It's the result of doing, instead of worrying about the "what ifs."

Fear is powerful. It's paralyzing and can keep you from asking what you want to ask, saying what you want to say, and doing what you want to do. It zaps your power if you let it. But, you can take control over your fear.

Familiar is comfortable, but It often means you miss out on a lot of amazing experiences, as well as the potential meet some amazing people. Here is a key to overcoming fear. Focusing on what you may be missing out on can help you get past being too afraid to try. Be more afraid of missing opportunities than of making mistakes. Be reasonable – i.e., don't walk out in front of heavy traffic without looking – but don't stand in the middle of the crosswalk trembling, or you'll get run over.

I've got some good news. You don't even have to really *be* confident. You just have to *seem* confident. The fact is that if you can pretend you're not afraid, you will soon truly no longer be afraid. Having enough faith to at least try is what gives you confidence.

Here's another secret. Even that best looking, wealthiest guy in the room has experienced fear. He has shortcomings and fears that he focuses on as well.

How others perceive us is largely determined by how we make others see us. If you are shy and timid around the beautiful woman who works in your building, then she is going to see you as shy and timid. If you smile, look her in the eye, and make a friendly comment, she is going to see you as the nice, friendly guy who works in her building. And chances are she will smile and say hello – or more – the next time she sees you.

Here are some additional ways to appear more confident:

1. Practice good posture. Standing up straight signifies strength and purpose.
2. Smile. We talked about this is Chapter 1, but in case you forgot (or skipped) that part, women love it when a man smiles. It also convinces others that you are happy, healthy, and even wise.
3. Make eye contact. When you look a person in the eyes, it indicates that you're strong and have nothing to hide.
4. Lean slightly forward. When you are sitting or standing, leaning forward demonstrates energy and forthrightness, which in turn signals strength and willingness. It also moves your energy forward. Be careful though, because leading forward too much may seem aggressive.
5. Have a firm handshake. If you are in a situation where you meet a woman and shake her hand, do it firmly – not limply, and not so hard it's painful – and look her in the eye. This says all kinds of positive things about you. You're not afraid. You're friendly. You're engaging.

It's natural to be nervous. When you feel those nerves start to creep up, remind yourself that you've felt this way before; and you survived. Ask yourself what's the worst thing that could happen, and what are the chances of that.

On the other hand, don't act cocky. Bragging about your conquests actually sends the message that you are insecure and are just trying to convince everyone else how great you are.

Additional Ways to Build Your Confidence

- **Inventory the things you do well.** It can be as simple as being able to tie a tie and anything from helping your elderly neighbor, to fixing a mean pot roast, to having a likable laugh. Everyone does something well, and building confidence begins by focusing on at least one thing. If you can't think of one thing, you're probably not looking at yourself objectively. Ask a friend or even your mother to help you think of something that you do well.

- **Work on developing your personal style**. Figure out what looks good on you or allows you to make your own personal statement that makes you feel good about how you look. Feeling good about you look is a great way to boost your confidence. That being said, on your first date, it's best to wear something you know you looks good and that is comfortable rather than something much different from what you would normally wear. New clothes may be uncomfortable, and that can be distracting or make you more nervous. The same holds true for wearing new shoes.

- **Do something good for someone else.** Helping others can build your confidence, because the other person appreciates you for doing something nice. Not to mention it just feels good, which boosts serotonin and helps you stay positive. Being appreciated boosts self-esteem.

- **Challenge yourself.** Try doing something you didn't think you could do – trying a new exercise, cooking a fancy meal, talking to the lady down the hall. Even if you don't do a great job, you can be proud that you accomplished something out of your comfort zone.

- **Revel in your accomplishments.** It is actually okay to feel a sense of accomplishment by doing something you know you can do well. It's a good start for building confidence. Just as feelings of incompetence seem to spread, so, too, can more positive feelings.

Chapter 3: Are You Ready to Date?

When it comes to dating, finding the right person really needs to happen at the right time, otherwise you may be asking for a disaster. (And finding the wrong person at the wrong time is just – well - wrong.)

What are the wrong times?

1. When you are feeling needy. "Needing" someone implies you are dependent on the person in order to feel happy and whole. That's not a healthy way to begin a relationship. Dating when you are needy will likely leave you in a lopsided relationship that will eventually burn out and leave you in a worse situation than you were in to begin with. Not only will you have the original issues that left you feeling needy, you'll also have the pain of a failed relationship.

2. When you've suffered a recent loss. Whether it's a relative, a friend, or even a pet, death and loss often triggers the desire to not be alone. Unfortunately, dates are not band-aids. Dating someone before you've had time to heal can easily ruin a good thing.

3. You've lost your job, your home, or something else that needs to take priority. If you've lost your job, or your home, you need to set priorities. Finding a job or a place to live is more important than finding a date. You need to take care of your basic needs before you focus on someone else. Besides, you don't want to be down in the dumps because you're unemployed when you go out on that first date.

4. You are absolutely swamped with work or another project. On the one hand, a single date doesn't require that much time. It could be a much-needed break. However, finding that first date can take a while, and if you want more than one date, you've got to be able to commit some time to the relationship. That's not going to work if you are so busy you don't have time for your date.

4. You're on the rebound. If you just broke up with someone, connecting with someone else is likely just a way to prove to yourself you're still attractive to women. It's not fair to your date or to you; and these relationships rarely work out.

5. You're depressed. Everyone feels sad and alone at times. But, if you're struggling with major depression, it's best to work on getting yourself better before you drag someone else into the equation. If you need professional help, by all means, get it.

When is the Right Time?

If you haven't figured it out already, the best time to start dating is when things are going well, already. You have friends, you have a job, you're relatively happy with who you are, you aren't dwelling on your exes, and so on.

Also, the happier you are, the more confident you are, and the more attractive a date you will be.

What's Your Type?

Even if you've figured out it's the right time to start dating, there's still some work that needs to be done. To be most successful, you should first figure out what makes you tick - and what type of woman you are attracted to and why.

Before you start to figure out the type of woman you are interested in, make a list of the things that interest you, and the things that really grate on your nerves.

For example, do you love to hike? Write it down. Are you an animal lover? Write it down. Can't stand it when people talk in movies? Write it down.

Next, think about your fantasy date. What does she look like? What does she do for a living? What is her personality like? Is she loud or shy? Serious or silly? High maintenance or down-to-earth? Be as detailed as possible.

Next, compare your lists. Is your fantasy date compatible with your personality? If you want a woman who is mysterious, but you hate surprises — maybe that's not a great match. Or if you are spontaneous and she likes to plan ahead, there could be problems. If you want to travel the world and she wants to settle down and have kids, again, this is probably going to lead to problems.

Also, do you want to date someone similar to you, or someone who will complement you?

A smart exercise to do at this point is to write out a pretend personal ad – just for fun. Unlike a real personal ad, use as many words as you need to. Write down who you are and what you're looking for; then step back and see if those two mesh. Look for compatible or complimentary characteristics.

Stepping back, maybe you're not really sure what you want in a date, and that's OK. You can still try to figure out who you are and what makes you tick. This will also help send up red flags later when you actually do begin dating.

Part 2: Finding and Having Your First Date

Chapter 4: Dating in the Modern World

With the many new changes in technology over the past 20 or so years, the dating process has drastically changed.

Whereas dating was once primarily for the purpose of finding someone to settle down with, marriage doesn't play near the role it did just a few years ago. Dating has changed; roles have changed; sexuality has changed; marriage has changed; even procreation issues have changed.

Online Dating

Online dating has both benefits and disadvantages. For one, the number of potential dates has significantly increased - and so have the choices. It has provided opportunities for people to meet who might not have otherwise found each other. It also helps people find dates who share common likes, interests, and beliefs.

On the downside, looking for a date is time consuming, addictive, and misleading.
When putting together profiles or chatting with potential dates, it's easy to exaggerate to make yourself sound different than you really are. It's marketing; and in some ways, the whole process is a fantasy. We will delve into this more in the next chapter.

Texting or Messaging

Talking on the phone is a dying art, as people tend to communicate by text or a messaging program. This kind of communication gives a false impression in that people are able to edit before sending. Additionally, other than the use of emojis, there's no real sense of tone, which can lead to miscommunication when relying on type alone.

Long Distance Relationships

People who live far apart are meeting online. The problem with long distance relationships is that, again, they are largely fantasy. For one, you don't see all the bad sides of the other person like you do when you meet in person. It's easy to spend more time fantasizing about being together when you're not actually together. When you finally meet up in person, you may spend most of that time in the bedroom rather than actually getting to know each other slowly.

Online Chatting

Much like texting, chatting online causes problem for married couples even when the conversations are not suggestive. It's easy to become emotionally attached to someone in a chat room. Much like everything else we've discussed in this chapter, chatting sets up a fantasy world.

Cell Phones

We are in a day where people are literally addicted to their phones. A quick note: if you are on a date, put it on vibrate. Do not pull it out and look at your social media in the middle of dinner.

Who Pays?

As gender roles are changing, it's difficult to know for sure whether you should pay for the date, or if she will be offended if you do. That being said, when in doubt, be a gentleman. At least offer to pay or you will look cheap. If she insists on paying, let her – or tell her she can pick up the tip.

Safety

For the sake of your date, as well as yourself, if you are meeting your date for the first time, meet her in a public place. Make sure someone knows where you will be, and don't give her your home address until you know her better.

Meeting Your Match in Today's Dating Scene

Learning to successfully date is a process and takes practice. Look at each date – good or bad – as a learning practice. Keep track of things that go well and not so well, then tweak as you go along.

Dating should be fun and exciting. If you find dating is becoming taxing, take a break for a while. Besides, sometimes the best relationships show up when you're not actively looking.

Chapter 5: Online Dating & Dating Apps

If you have tried online dating, you probably have found it's not as easy or effective as you'd hoped it would be. The women you are interested in don't respond, and the ones that do are not the ones you want.

Beautiful women on dating sites get overwhelmed by the amount of guys who are interested in them. You've got a lot of competition and it can be hard to stand out.

The key is to think like and brand yourself as an alpha male. What does that mean?

In Chapter 1, we talked about what women find attractive in men. One of the main traits is confidence. Alpha males come across as confident. In chapter 2, we talked about how to practice building confidence. Now we're going to talk about how to exude confidence online.

Imagine a beautiful woman on a dating site looking at different male profiles. You see two profiles next to each other, both are about equal in physical attractiveness. One labels his profile as "NiceGuy" and the other is "LeaderofthePack."

Nice Guy's headline said "Sweet lonely guy looking for love." His profile picture is him sitting on his couch holding a beer.

Leader's headline says "Warning: Excitement Ahead." His profile picture is him holding a glass of wine, toasting the camera, with a mountainous backdrop behind him.

Can you guess which one she chooses?

Whose message do you think she's going to return?

When a beautiful woman sees your profile picture (and remember - you've only got a brief moment to make an impression) she's picturing what a date, or even a lifetime, might be like with you. Does she want to hang out on your couch and play video games? Or does she want romance and adventure? Make your profile picture reflect the desires of her fantasies.

Show her you're an alpha male – someone who is interesting and exciting and who will make her life more amazing.

That being said, you've got to be subtle. You need to show her how cool you are, not tell her.

Your profile can illustrate your alpha qualities through the words you choose. Don't just say what you do for a living. Share that you are a go-getter who works hard so that you enjoy the finest rewards that life has to offer. That description illustrates both excitement and stability, both of which are important to women.

Choose photos that show you doing things. Make sure you are the center of attention in any photo you choose. Research has even found that women are drawn to photos where a man is surrounded by smiling women.

When you message a woman online, make sure you sound confident. Never apologize for your looks. Be proud no matter what. Remember those "Most Interesting Man in the World" commercials. He's not necessarily the best looking man in the world. He's the most interesting man, and he is the center of attention.

Let Her Know You Are Successful

Security is important to a woman. You want her to know you have a job, your own place, and your own vehicle. But you can't blurt out "I make X amount of dollars a year" and expect a woman to be impressed. (Some may be, but probably not the right type.)

Instead, you need to let her know about your lifestyle, and that will indicate your resources. Include descriptions or photos of trips you've taken or home improvement projects you've completed. Mention what you like about your job.

Here's a tip: if you own a pet, be sure to include it. Ideally if you own a dog, you can include something about hiking with your dog. Owning a pet shows you're responsible. Plus a lot of women just really like pets.

Interestingly, a recent study found that although liking cats is attractive, specifically mentioning your own cat is not.

Loyalty

Women want to know you're loyal, but they don't want to read "I'm loyal." Again, you can't just tell her; you need to show her.

Loyalty can be connected to family, so if you mention going to your niece's ballet recital or having Sunday dinner with your family, you're showing that you are loyal and family is important. If you have kids already, tell a funny parenting story. (Just keep the discussion of your kids brief.)

Which Sites Should You Use?

Now that you understand how to maximize your online dating profile, you need to choose which sites and apps you want to use.

There are thousands of dating apps and sites out there - and new ones are popping up all the time.

Online dating is time consuming, so you really need to figure out where you can maximize your effort and cut out those sites that aren't a good fit for you.

For most guys, unless they live in a major city, it's typically smartest to use a mainstream site like Tinder or Match.com. More popular sites have larger dating pools, and more options for potential dates.

Here are some you might want to consider:

- **Match.com** has the largest number of users and focuses on both brains and beauty. There is a monthly fee, which is good because it means the women you find there are more serious about dating.

- **Tinder** is the most popular dating app in the U.S., and is a favorite for the younger (early 20's) crowd. Tinder is a swipe left or right app, so having a good quality photo is imperative.

- **Bumble** is similar to Tinder, with one big difference. Only females can initiate contact. The dating pool isn't as large as Tinder, but it attracts a higher quality, "meet the parents" kind of woman. Bumble is a good option.

- **OkCupid** is a good option if you're into women who have unique styles, such hipsters or goths, or even just those who are career driven. It's primarily popular with 18 to 34 year olds, but there are women of all ages. The basic accounts are free, but a premium account gives you some better features and the price is minimal.

- **CoffeeMeetsBagle (CMB)** really focuses on quality over quantity. Men receive 21 potential matches every day, and women receive a vetted group of about 5 men who have already said "yes" to her profile.

- **PlentyofFish (POF)** is the top free dating site, which means there are tons of users. However, you have to spend more time screening profiles since it is free.

There are also several niche sites for specific targets. The problem is they just don't attract the volume, so the dating pool is relatively small unless you live in a really big city. Some to try out though would be ChristianMingle.com, Jdate (a popular Jewish dating site), The League (for intelligent and successful people), and FarmersOnly.com.

Which Photos Should You Use?

Your online dating photos should:

- **Show you looking your best**. Your photos should not be blurry or grainy. It also shouldn't show you playing video games on your couch. You probably wouldn't approach a beautiful woman if you were wearing a filthy t-shirt and hadn't showered for days. A poor photo has a similar affect.
- **Communicate the right message.** Again, you're wanting to show that you are confident, in control, and a leader. Show photos that reflect your life (but not if your life is playing video games on the couch). Choose photos with your dog, with friends (make sure you're the center of attention), and of you partaking in whatever hobbies you may have.
- **Reinforce your profile.** Consistency is key. If your profile says you are an adventurer who loves the outdoors, but the pictures are all taken inside, it's going to look like you are making stuff up. If she feels like you aren't trustworthy, she's going to be uncomfortable meeting you in person.

A few more tips for taking photos:

- **Don't use a flash.** An OkCupid study found that flashes add 7 years to your perceived age online. The light also casts shadows on your face and highlights your flaws.
- **Include outdoor photos.** A study found that outdoor photos increase responses by about 20%. This may be because natural light is flattering. The best times to shoot are 60 minutes after dawn or 60 minutes before sunset.
- **Stand with your body at a 45 degree angle to the camera.** This is a power pose.
- **Consider having professional photos taken.** Just don't use all professional shots because it'll look like you're trying too hard. If you use a pro, don't use studio backgrounds. You want to have professional quality photos that don't look like you hired someone to take them. (If you have a work-related profile shot, that is OK to use.) Ideally, you want to change locations and outfits.
- **Choose between 3 and 7 pictures.** A collection of fewer than 3 pictures makes it hard to capture everything you want a potential date to grasp about your personality. More than 7 is just too many.
- **Have a female friend or relative help you pick out your photos.**

Writing Your Profile

Profiles vary based on the site or app, but typically they allow for 100 to 500 words. Keep in mind that she's probably reading on her phone, so it's better to keep it short, punchy, and easy to digest quickly. She's going to be skimming, not reading every word.

That being said, don't get too attached to your profile's wording. You are going to rank better if you regularly update it.

Step 1: The Name

Your photo is going to be the focal point of your profile, but your username is also right up there. Use it to make yourself stand out.

Using your first name does make you sound approachable, even though it's not very creative. Just don't become David12345. If your real name is common, you may be better of using a clever name.

Research has found that women are drawn to intangible qualities like intelligence, risk taking, and bravery. Use that data when coming up with a name.

- NoRiskNoReward
- AlwaysAhead

Make sure your username is positive. Don't expect her to fall for LonelyGuy405. Also, don't be aggressive or crude; NineIncher or Hot4You are not appealing.

Your Headline

Depending on the site, your photo and username may appear next to a headline. These are typically a short sentence, but they are important attention-getters.

Your profile headline should pique her interest. If you can make her stop and think, she may look longer at your photo. Studies have found that the longer she looks at your photo, the more she'll like you.

Try to create a headline that makes her curious like "Hope you have your passport."

Your Profile

- Spend 70% of your profile focused on you and what you have to offer. The remaining 30% is on what you are looking for.
- Pay attention to spelling, punctuation, and grammar.
- Be honest. You may feel the need to exaggerate a bit, but remember you will hopefully meet her.
- Aim for 250 to 300 words.
- Don't use foul or offensive language.
- Don't say anything negative.
- Don't mention past relationships.
- Don't make it all about her or you will appear desperate.
- Don't stuff your profile with a list of adjectives. It's not original or effective.
- Don't be cocky. Don't tell how great you are. Show how great you are. Share stories, etc., that illustrate that you are adventurous or caring or loyal or fun. As an example, rather than just saying you love to travel, describe a trip you've taken.

Here is a formula that usually works well.

First paragraph – Hook her with a personal story.

Second paragraph – Explain what you do for a living, but make it interesting.

Third paragraph – Talk about hobbies and interests.

Fourth Paragraph – Describe what type of woman you are interested in meeting.

If you have a website that shows off your hobbies or skills, link to that and let that tell how great you are.

When it comes to your job, try to describe something interesting that you do, not just that you are a store manager or work at a bank.

The good news is that once you create a profile, you can usually just kind of tweak and reuse it on multiple sites.

Crafting Your Message

Remember: Alpha Male.

Your goal is to make her want to pursue you. One big mistake is to be overly complimentary about how beautiful she is. Instead, your goal is to craft your message so that she feels she needs to prove she is worthy of your time.

Remember that women enjoy a good sense of humor, and a little humor can help make the conversation feel more relaxed and leave her wanting to respond.

We'll talk more about dating apps in the next chapter, but just know that dating sites generally move at a little slower pace. She may take a day or two to respond, and you may want to do the same. That being said, you don't want to wait so long that she moves on.

Your opening message should always ask an engaging question. Topics like food, travel, pop culture, hobbies, etc., generally work well. The questions need to be hypothetical and fun, not personal.

Here are a few things to remember about online messages:

- Use humor and creativity to pique her interest.
- Keep it short.
- Use proper spelling, grammar, and punctuation.
- Ask a question so it's easy for her to respond.

On the other hand, you don't want to do the following:

- Tell her how gorgeous she is.
- Use a bunch of emojis, etc.
- Be cryptic by using random humor.
- Recommend going off the site in the first message. She needs to be comfortable with you first.

Research has found that you can expect to get one response for every 114 messages you send out. These suggestions, however, can help you increase those odds.

For one, copy and paste your icebreaker messages.

You can also design an icebreaker message based on certain words. For example, if you like to travel and you want a partner who also likes to travel, write something like this:

"I see that you're someone who likes spontaneity and adventure. So tell me this. If you were given an all-expense-paid trip to anywhere in the world but you had to leave within the next hour, where would you go?"

By using the advanced search function and entering the word "travel," you suddenly have a ton of prospects for your icebreaker message.

Keep track of which messages work and which don't.

Asking Her Out

Although you may be connecting with a woman online, it's a little trickier when it comes to actually going out.

Here are some signs that she is interested in you:

- Her messages answer your questions and then some; and they are somewhat long.
- She's using exclamation points, etc.
- She's asking you questions, as well.

Generally, you can ask her out after she's sent you two or three messages. You don't want to seem too eager, but you don't want to wait too long and have her move on.

Dating Apps: A Few Differences

The rules for dating apps are similar to those for online dating sites, except everything moves faster.

Because Tinder is the top dating app in the U.S., we're going to use it as our example.

Tinder's huge popularity is due largely to its ability to give instant gratification. With Tinder, people anonymously look at potential dates' photos and a very brief bio, then either swipe left (reject) or swipe right (possible match).

Here are a few things to keep in mind:

1. Your bio needs to be no more than 3 sentences.
2. Tinder offers a free version and a premium version. The premium version has added benefits, including unlimited swiping
3. If you use the free version, you only get a limited number of swipes per day. Keep in mind that the first 10 or so swipes have already swiped right on your photo, so keep an open mind.
4. There are lots of fake accounts that try to spam you. If you see some truly sexy babe that looks out of place, it's probably a fake account. Don't fall for it.

Your App Profile

Swiping apps like Tinder and Bumble are primarily photo driven, but that doesn't mean you don't need a strong profile. In fact, a study showed that male Tinder users received four times as many matches when they included a profile. (Some only use photos.)

She most likely won't respond to a message from you if you only use photos. And a strong profile may persuade her to check out your photos.

App profiles are shorter than online profiles, and that makes it more difficult. Again, you want to sound confident. Also, you can't simply cut and paste your profiles on apps like you can for online dating sites. Tinder and Bumble users are generally quite different.

Your goals for your profile are to:

1. Get her attention.
2. Make her want to learn more about you.
3. Make her smile.

Follow the same guidelines for your profile that you did on the dating sites, only make it shorter. Even though Tinder is known for being more casual and a place to "hook up" more than "date," don't be sleezy. Also, practice good grammar, etc. Stay classy.

It's OK to use slightly cocky humor on Tinder. On Bumble, remember that women are the ones who have to make the first move, so class and tact is really important there. Practicing good behavior will make your profile stand out, as well.

Again, use (brief) descriptive examples rather than just a lazy list of adjectives. You want her to be impressed by how interesting you are and want to know more about you. If she returns your message, you're off to a good start.

Dating App Messages

For dating apps, you've got to keep the momentum going. Apps are fast. You want the conversation to progress quickly with the goal of moving off the app – i.e., communicating other ways, such as the phone, email, or even a meet up – as quickly as possible.

App messages have a short shelf life and if you don't keep it moving, she may move on.

For example, on CoffeeMeetsBagel, you only have 24 hours to decide whether to like or pass on your match. Once you both like each other, your message disappears after eight days. On Bumble, only women can send the first message, and you have to respond within 24 hours. You get the idea.

While Tinder has no time limit, there's tons of competition. If she's a regular "swipe right," she's going to get lots of messages from other guys. You've got to move it or lose it.

Again, your initial message needs to pique her interest so she will respond. No lewd pickup lines or boring "What's up?" messages. With a little creativity and effort, she will actually respond.

Rather than just a "hey" – which leaves the ball in her court – come up with an icebreaker. Again, your icebreaker should create a positive emotional response and ask a question so she will respond.

Humor is an especially effective way to get her attention. Animated gifs also are 30% more likely to get responses. If humor isn't your thing, try asking her a question that's easy to answer but fun to think about. The "where would you go if you had a free trip but only an hour to leave" question from before is still a good one.

Travel is always a great opener because the conversation can continue no matter what she answers. Keep the conversation flowing by asking another question every time she responds.

After you've gotten about 10 responses, it's probably safe to ask to take the conversation elsewhere – email, phone, or a date.

Chapter 6: Where to Find a Potential Date

This chapter includes some good – and some not-so-good – places to meet women in person. These are just suggestions, and certainly do not include all the possible places to meet potential dates.

However, keep these things in mind:

- **Stay aware.** Children are taught not to talk to strangers for good reason. And unfortunately, men and women alike still have to be cautious of strangers as they get older. Before you approach a woman, make sure you do so gently and with civility.
- **Stay considerate.** If someone is brave enough to approach you first and you're not interested, unless they are super scary or inappropriate, be polite when you say no.
- **Stay patient.** If you knew you'd meet the woman of your dreams in five years and you'd live happily ever after for another 50 years, would you be willing to wait? Yes, of course you would. So if you're looking for the woman of your dreams, try to think of dating as just a matter of time. If you can consider dating fun, it will help you seem more attractive as well.

When it comes to finding a date, the best options are well-lit, not too loud, safe, comfortable, and where you have an interest in whatever is going on. If it is a place that you enjoy, it will be easier for you to strike up a conversation. Keep your approach light and friendly.

Here are some good options:

- **Educational classes.** College courses, adult education classes, or art/hobby classes are all good places to meet people.

- **Your neighborhood.** There may be some very datable people who live in your neighborhood. Pay attention to who you run across in your area. You may even already be acquainted with one another, which makes the situation less scary.
- **Parties.** A party can be a good place to meet someone. And you both probably know at least one or more of the same people at the party, which makes conversation less stressful.
- **Grocery stores.** Again, shopping at the same local market offers familiarity, which makes the situation less threatening.
- **Laundromats.** It's easy to strike up a conversation when you're both stuck at the boring laundromat.
- **Bookstores or libraries.** A lot of bookstores (and even some libraries) have big, comfortable chairs and jazzy music playing in the background. It's a great place to strike up a casual conversation. (Just don't be too loud at the library!)
- **Places of worship.** A lot of churches and other religions institutions have singles departments and events, making it easier for people with shared beliefs to meet.
- **Volunteer activities.** We already talked about volunteer activities being a good way to build self-confidence. It can also be a good place to find a date. Just be sure to pick something that you care about and enjoy. Along those same lines, volunteering for a political campaign is another place to build self-confidence, potentially meet someone with shared beliefs, and help an important cause.
- **Gyms.** Again, there's a familiarity with the gym. You see a lot of the same people every time you go, and you are all doing similar things. Striking up a conversation is relatively easy. Just be friendly and slow if you approach a potential date at the gym.
- **Individual sports.** Running, cycling, golfing and so on can all be considered individual sports, but they often have strong communities. It's easy to join area groups online or meet people at events. You also may pass some of the same people

regularly when you're out jogging. A quick wave and a smile can be the start of a potential date.

Getting Set Up

Your friends, family, coworkers, etc., may have a single friend they'd like you to meet. While it may seem awkward, this can actually be a good way to find a date. Hopefully, they won't set you up with someone who is completely crazy. Just be prepared to be drilled about the date. You may also hurt your friend's feelings if you decide not to ask their suggested date out again.

Not-So-Great Options

- **The Office.** Not only will everyone know about your date, there may be a no-dating rule within your office. Interoffice romances are just a bad idea. That being said, dating someone who works in your same building but not for your same company is not a bad idea.
- **Bars.** This is obviously where a lot of people meet dates. The problem is that it's dark and almost everyone has been drinking, which alters perception. Plus, bars are too noisy to talk in.
- **Singles Dances or Speed Dating Events.** These are both events designed to help singles connect, so what's wrong with them? The problem is that these kinds of activities are created to pair you off with someone you may have no interest in. That being said, as long as you can go and have fun and don't put a ton of pressure on yourself, these events are fine. If nothing else, they can give you practice in striking up conversations with potential dates in the future.

Chapter 7: Your Approach

The Eyes Have It

Making eye contact is crucial, especially for a strong first impression. You have to connect with the eyes to truly connect.

There's a fine line between being attractive and being creepy when it comes to eye contact. Lock eyes for a brief moment, but don't stare. If you feel awkward making eye contact, the good news is it's an easy thing to practice.

Any time you are walking somewhere other people are – the mall, the grocery story, the park – make relaxed eye contact with everyone you pass. Obviously, you aren't going to be relaxed if you are new to this, but the more you practice, the easier it will become. One trick is to imagine you already know and like that person. This can help you feel more confident and relaxed.

An important reminder: look at her eyes. Don't look at your shoes. Don't talk to her breasts.

From Your Mouth . . .

After the initial eye contact, the next step is to actually say something.

Let's look at what generally works and what doesn't.

Do:

- **Be sincere.** This requires meaning what you say, and it has to be focused on the other person. Unfortunately, this is not

something you can practice in front of a mirror — because then it's not sincerity.
- **Be honest.** Don't try to make yourself into someone you're not. Don't pretend to like things you don't like, or that you're great at things you're not. However, being honest doesn't mean baring your soul, and it doesn't mean telling your date things you don't like about her.
- **Be friendly.** Again, a genuine smile goes a long way.
- **Be positive.** This falls back on the things that women like; and positivity is a big plus.
- **Be attentive.** Actually listening to what the other person is (or persons are, if you're talking with a group) saying and interacting by asking questions is really attractive.
- **Touch.** This is a tricky one, especially in today's world. Playful touch can be a turn on, but be cautious; and if you do touch, make it non-threatening. A quick brush of the arm. Bump knees. Stay away from anything that could be taken as sexual.
- **Make the first move.** And by "move," I simply mean find someone and talk to her. Don't just wait for someone to come flirt with you. Worst case scenario, she says no. And while your ego may feel a little wounded, you're really no worse off than you were before you asked. Rejection is only one person's opinion, and you never know all the circumstances behind the no, either.
- **Compliment — but be genuine.** Don't use a cheesy pick up line to let her know you think she's beautiful. But if she has a beautiful smile, it's OK to let her know it. Women generally like to be complimented on things above the neck: their eyes, hair, and smile. Not on their "rockin body." Also, compliment once. That's enough. If you keep going on and on about her eyes or her smile, it's gets to be a bit creepy.

Don't:

- **Be slimy.** There are a few guys who can get away with being slick, but most can't. It's better not to come across as a creepy car salesman type.
- **Be obscene.** Guys tend to think they can pick up women by being lewd, and it rarely-to-never works.
- **Be too stupid or silly.** Funny is one thing, silly – like straws up the nose or being obnoxious on the dance floor – is just childish (and weird).
- **Be negative.** Gossiping, complaining, whining, and being argumentative just really aren't attractive qualities.
- **Use cheesy pick-up lines.** "If I said you had a beautiful body, would you hold it against me?" Umm…no. That's not going to work. However, going over and telling a woman that her beautiful smile was distracting you…that could actually work.

Improving Your Odds

When asking for a date, keep these things in mind:

Have your first date on a weeknight, not the weekend. People often have plans on the weekend, but weeknights are not as busy and you've got a better chance of getting a "yes." Mondays are usually just bad days, so avoid asking for a Monday night date.

Don't ask, "Would you like to go out sometime?" This question leaves you no options. If she says no, there's no way out. If she says yes then you have to ask her out.

Instead, have a plan. "There's a new restaurant I've been wanting to try. Would you be interested in joining me Wednesday or Thursday night?" Providing a specific offer and a choice of days gives you some room to negotiate. It also allows your potential date a moment to think about her response rather than getting caught completely off guard.

Always give your date options. Whether it's the day, time, or location, giving your date options improves the chances of it going well. Otherwise, if you plan the whole date out and she doesn't like your plan, it's all on you.

If it is your first date, you can ask if she's more comfortable meeting you at the date's location or if she'd like you to pick her up. This shows you are considerate and sensitive to the concerns that women may have about a date being dangerous. You may know you are not dangerous, but she may feel a little uncomfortable getting in the car with someone she just met.

Don't Plan the Date Too Soon or Too Far Away

A general rule is to ask for your first date a week to 10 days in advance. The exception is if things are going well and you want to ask her to go get a cup of coffee, or an ice cream cone, or something along those lines.

It's also better to ask her out in the moment, while you are talking and have the courage, as opposed to later.

The Invitation: Sending the Message

When it comes to actually asking for the date, you have options. When possible, it's best to ask when you are close together – e.g., face to face, as opposed to over the phone.

Here are some options, which can be adapted for your particular situation.

- **Ask in person.** This is the best way to ask someone for a date because you get to see each other face to face, which allows

you to read body language and get other clues about the experience. Based on her reaction, you can adjust. On the downside, it's the most nerve-racking technique.
- **Over the phone.** You aren't able to see her body language, but she also can't see yours – sweaty palms and all. If she does not pick up, don't ask her out over voicemail. Plus you'll never know if she actually heard the message or not.
- **Text or email.** Remember the reasons not to leave a voicemail? Apply these to why you shouldn't leave a text or email. It looks cowardly and lazy.
- **Through a friend.** You aren't in middle school. Don't have a friend ask for you.

Dealing with a "No"

If the woman says no, you can ask if another time or place would be better. Often people are just really busy and would be willing to take a rain check on that date. You can offer to give her your number and ask her to call when she's ready (just know that may be never). You can also suggest you call her in a couple of weeks to see how things are going.

Getting a Phone Number

Ask in a friendly way. "I'd really like to stay in touch. Can I get your phone number?"

One way to make a good impression is to say something like, "I know that a beautiful woman like you has to be cautious, so if you'd prefer, how about I give you my number instead?"

An important note: if you're not interested, don't ask for her number.

Making the Follow-Up Call

Also, guys often think they have to wait to call a woman they are interested in so they don't look too needy. Realistically, it's OK to call the next day or to even ask her out on a date. Just don't stay on the phone long and keep the conversation casual.

Chapter 8: Planning the First Date

The purpose of a first date should be to get to know each other without breaking your bank account.

First Things First

Keep in mind that while a date should ideally be relaxing and enjoyable, it may not be. But it doesn't have to be nerve-wracking either.

Here are some general rules for increasing the likelihood of having an enjoyable first date.

1. Do something you enjoy. Don't pick an activity that you hate because you think your date will enjoy it. This might be good to do later on, but not on the first date. Hopefully, if it's something she hates, she will let you know.

2. Do something you can afford. Don't spend a ton of money you don't have in order to try to impress your date. There's no way you can keep that kind of experience up, which makes you look cheap later. Plus, you never know if your date will like it, or if you really like her enough to justify that kind of expense. Also, even if you can easily afford to fly her across the world, don't suggest something too far out of her comfort zone until she gets to know you better.

3. Do something that doesn't require buying new clothes. As discussed earlier in this book, new clothes are often uncomfortable, and the more comfortable you are – within reason (i.e., no sweats at dinner) – the more enjoyable your date will be. Wear something that looks and feels good on you, and that you feel good in.

4. Pick an activity where you can talk. The old "dinner and a movie" is fine once you get to know each other, but watching a movie isn't really a "together" activity.

5. Pick a location that's conveniently located. You don't want to plan a date that's far away from where you both live. And even things like parking downtown can be an issue – especially if you're taking separate cars.

6. Make sure there's time to get to know each other. That's the most important reason for your first date, so there needs to be down time and you need to pick a location, like a restaurant, that's not super noisy.

7. Don't include tagalongs. Your date should be just the two of you, not you and your family or friends.

8. Keep the date short. Ideally, your date won't run more than a couple of hours. If it's enjoyable, you will both look forward to the next date. If your date is miserable, at least it will be over soon.

9. Limit your alcohol consumption. A glass of wine might help calm your nerves (or hers), but don't overdo it. You don't want to look like you have a drinking problem, you don't want to act like a fool, and you don't want to drive drunk.

Good First Date Options

1. Amusement Parks, Fairs, or Carnivals. Note, we're not talking Disney World or other big parks that can easily break the bank. These are your small, home-town kind of parks or fairs where you can have fun, get to know each other, eat ice cream, and so on.

2. Museums or Art Galleries. Even if this is not really your "thing," museums and galleries are quiet, laid-back, and allow you to slowly meander and chat while getting to know each other. It's a great way to get to know about each other's tastes and interests. A lot of museums also have a place where you can eat on your date.

3. Walks or hikes. Assuming the weather cooperates, you can go for a walk in variety of places, including the zoo, botanical gardens, and popular (and well populated) trails.

4. Street fairs or local indoor tradeshows. Again, this is an affordable option that allows you to hang out and get to know about each other's interests.

5. Outdoor activities. As long as it's not too hot or too cold, doing things outside is a nice, fun option. Picnics, frisbee golf, outdoor fairs, zoos, and so on are all good options.

Keep an eye on the local events that are coming to your area and plan accordingly.

Choosing a Restaurant

Going out to eat is probably the most common first date option, but you can make it special.

- **Go to a coffeehouse instead of a restaurant.** Coffeehouses are relaxed, comfortable, and generally aren't pushing you to finish up your meal and get out.
- **Choose an interesting locally-owned restaurant.** Put some effort into researching options and go to a unique, hidden-away restaurant rather than your traditional chains. Lunches and brunches are also nice options.

- **Doublecheck the noise level.** If it's a new restaurant where you've never eaten, you may want to pop in before you plan the date to see how loud it is. It's hard to get to know each other if you can't hear each other.
- **Space.** Again, this may be one of those things you should check out before you go. You don't want a restaurant where you'll be seated almost directly next to another party.
- **Choose something affordable.** In most communities, there are lots of hole-in-the-wall options that are also affordable. Make sure you can afford both the meal, plus appetizers, desserts, and drinks. If that's going to be a problem, choose someplace that doesn't serve extras or alcohol.
- **Avoid trendy new spots.** These can be loud, expensive, and require a long wait. If your first date goes well, you can visit these kinds of places together in the future.

Chapter 9: Getting Ready for Your Date

It's time to get ready for you date.

Even if you are nervous – and you probably are – try to stay positive. Remember, again, that it's just a date. Try to have fun. Now, let's get you ready.

Making a good first impression

It takes two seconds or less to take in someone's appearance, meaning you've only got about two seconds to make a good first impression. Make those two seconds count.

Hopefully, you've already found a comfortable style that suits you, so pick out an outfit that you will feel confident in.

You are probably going to be nervous, and that means you will probably perspire. Try to find an outfit that is not too hot and that doesn't show sweat stains. Pick a shirt that is breathable, and loose in the armpits and back. This may seem obvious, but make sure whatever you choose to wear is appropriate for whatever you will be doing on the date.

Here are some things to think about:

1. What do I look good in? Is there an outfit that you wear that you always get complimented on? If not, or you're not sure what looks good on you, try on an outfit and look at yourself from head to toe in the mirror. Or have a friend come help you.
2. Pick a color that suits you. If you aren't sure, a neutral like black or grey is a good choice.
3. Pick a fabric that doesn't wrinkle.

4. Choose something that fits well and that you are comfortable it. You can test the fit by dropping a penny on the floor then bending over to pick it up. If your clothes are too tight, you'll feel it.

Finally, don't skip the details. Press your shirt collar. Shine your shoes. Make sure your tags are tucked in. Look for loose threads. Make sure your socks match.

Practice Good Hygiene

Hopefully this is a given, but in addition to picking out a clean outfit, you need to make sure you are clean as well.

Freshen your breath. Shave. Comb your hair. Put on deodorant.

Cologne is probably OK, but keep it to a minimum. A lot of people have allergies and perfumes and colognes are irritants. So if you want to wear cologne and you aren't sure if she has allergies, spritz it into the air then walk through it rather than splashing it directly on you.

In the wild kingdom, the sense of smell plays a huge role in mating. Don't underestimate the power of the nose. Any time you smell something, it triggers the olfactory nerves, activating the emotional (limbic) center of the brain.

Just like in the wild, humans also release pheromones through natural secretions of the body that send signals to members of the opposite sex. Poor hygiene interferes with this whole process.

Women generally don't care for the smell of sweat. Make sure you select an antiperspirant/deodorant that works for you. You can actually also apply antiperspirant to the palms of your hands if you're concerned about having sweaty palms.

If you need a haircut, try getting it a day or two before the big date rather than the day of.

Here are some other hygienic things you need to do before your date:

- Take a shower
- Wash your ears
- Wash Your hair
- Brush your teeth
- Floss your teeth
- Shave
- Clip or file your nails
- Apply antiperspirant
- Make sure your clothes are clean

Picking up or Meeting Your Date

Make sure you are ready on time. Running late can make your date, who is probably already anxious, more nervous. If you tend to be late, plan to leave an extra 30 minutes before you need to. Limit or reschedule errands that you need to run on the same day as your date.

If you are picking up your date, make sure your car is clean and fueled up. Empty out the ashtray, throw away any trash or loose items, and wipe off the dash. Spritz air freshener so that it smells fresh. Vacuum if needed.

Swing by the ATM the day before your date just in case you need cash. Ideally, you will have a few dollar bills available in case you need to tip someone.

If you aren't familiar with the location or how long it will take to get there, practice driving there prior to your date. While GPS systems make it easier than ever before to find locations, it's still best to know exactly where you are going ahead of time. It just makes an already stressful situation less stressful for both of you.

Getting Your Insides Ready

Stress is your body's natural response to being overloaded by anxiety. Keep in mind that even too much of a good thing can cause stress.

When you are first getting to know someone, your senses are on overdrive trying to evaluate whether that person is a friend or enemy. Without you realizing it, you are relying on your intuition, past experiences, and current observations; and all of that causes stress until you determine it's OK to let your guard down.

We put up emotional walls, to keep people we don't really know from getting too close to us too quickly. It's not a bad thing. In fact, it's smart to be little cautious at first as long as you don't overdo it.

However, getting ready for a date can easily go from a little stress to stress overload if you aren't careful. You may find yourself running late, not knowing exactly what you want to wear, or not totally sure where you're going. Maybe your plans are having to change at the last minute because of weather or other issues. When one thing goes wrong, it often has a snowball effect.

One way to prevent your stress from sneaking up and taking over your preparations is to actively practice some stress relieving techniques before you get ready. Take at least 10 minutes and relax:

- Put on something comfortable.
- Choose a quiet room where the lighting and temperature are comfortable.
- Sit in a comfortable chair.
- Close and relax your eyes.
- If random or negative thoughts try to enter your mind, imagine those thoughts floating away on a fluffy cloud. (Sounds silly, but it works.)
- Listen to your body – your breathing, your heart pumping.
- Feel heavy in the chair.
- Breathe deeply – four counts in, hold for four, then four counts out.
- Repeat at least four times.

Next is implementing a progressive relaxation technique:

- Squeeze your toes tightly in a ball. Hold. Slowly release, then repeat.
- Roll each foot slowly in a clockwise circle. Then counterclockwise. Point toes. Flex. Repeat.
- Tense your thighs, hold, release, repeat.
- Tense your buns, hold, release, repeat.
- Tighten your abdominal muscles, hold, release, repeat.
- Lift your shoulders up towards your ears, hold, then slowly push them back down. Repeat.
- Clench your fists, flex your biceps, lower back down, relax, repeat.
- Extend your arms at shoulder length, then flex your hands so your palms face the wall and fingers point toward the ceiling. Press outward. Relax. Repeat.
- Turn your head to the left, then to the right as far as you can, keeping your shoulders pressed down. Repeat.
- Wrinkle your face into a ball, hold, relax, repeat.

By now you should feel relaxed. Before your open your eyes, it's time to visualize.

Visualization is a remarkable tool for relieving stress. Visualizing is essentially creating a safe place inside your head where you can always retreat to when you start to get too stressed. So to visualize:

- Think of a place that you been that makes you feel comfortable and happy. Picture as many details about that place as you can.
- Think of someone in your life who loves and cherishes you unconditionally. Picture that person walking toward you in your happy place. Watch as that person happily walks toward you. When that person is next to you, look into his or her eyes. Your special person already knows what you need.
- See a small point of bright, pure, warm light. Watch as that pinpoint of light expands and fills the entire space. You are comfortable and warm as you bathe in that light.
- Your special person is now leaving, but you aren't sad. That person and this place always stay with you.
- Keep your eyes closed, but slowly become aware of your surroundings.
- Slowly open your eyes and sit still for a moment. The calm you are feeling can now stay with you on your entire date if you let it.

Rather than feeling out of control, ready to call off the whole date, slow down and take a few deep breaths.

All Daters Get Nervous

Even with preparation and practice, dating can be nerve-racking. Here are some of the more common fears:

- What if I say the wrong thing? If you do, take a breath, apologize once, and explain that you are nervous. Then, let it go.
- What if I do the wrong thing? What if you spill your drink at dinner? Or trip and fall? Embarrassing, yes. Life changing, probably not. Everyone makes mistakes. Try to laugh it off.
- What if food gets caught in my teeth? Run your tongue across your teeth every once in a while, or excuse yourself to visit the bathroom and check your teeth. If it's really a concern, don't order foods like broccoli.
- What if I get an erection? Honestly, most women probably won't notice. If she does, she'll probably take it as a compliment.

A Quick Relaxation Technique

If you catch yourself feeling nervous, do the following:

1. Breathe deeply.
2. Relax your shoulders.
3. Place your hands flat on your knees (you can do this under the table where she won't see you) and stretch your fingers and palms.
4. Stretch your face. (You'll need to do this one in the bathroom.) Open your mouth and eyes as wide as you can, then hold, then release.
5. Control your mind. Just because your mind is subconsciously telling your body how to respond to stress doesn't mean you have to listen. Make your mind consciously tell your body to relax.

Affirmations

Another thing that can be effective is to practice affirmations – or thinking positive things about yourself in the present tense. These can also help any time you are feeling anxious. Examples include:

- I am a genuinely nice person.
- I am fun and interesting.
- I deserve to be happy and successful.
- A date is not a big deal.
- I will enjoy myself on my date and so will she.

Now that you are relaxed and ready, it's time to go have fun.

Chapter 10: Making Conversation

OK, you are now on your date. We've already talked about the need to relax, but it's really important. So again - at least try to relax. Remember that deep breathing is the best and most efficient way to calm your body down, and you can do it without anyone really noticing. So breathe!

Next it's time to talk.

Before your date, put together three questions to ask as ice breakers. Then, think of three things you want to share about yourself. Be prepared to talk about things like your job, things you like to do for fun, and maybe even a current event. These should just be short responses, not divulging every detail.

It's not a bad idea to have an informal guide of things you might want to talk about – including an opening line – planned out ahead of your date. Again, this can help calm your nerves.

Something that pretty much always works is to start out by telling your date she looks beautiful. You can be more specific – that dress really highlights the color of your eyes. Just don't compliment body parts located between the neck and her ankles. A compliment can help your date feel good about herself, which helps her relax, which in turn helps you relax. However, don't keep complimenting. That just comes across as weird.

Next it's time to start making small talk.

Small talk is really just being able to comfortably chat about simple, day to day issues without delving into things like politics, religion, or other controversial topics.

Here are some other good conversation starters:

- **The weather.** While it sounds silly, the weather is something everyone in your area can relate to.
- **Your location.** Wherever you are on your date, you can ask if she's been there before. Comment on what's going on around you. Share the experience together.
- **Friends you both may know.** Don't gossip though.
- **Pop culture.**
- **Recent news.** Just don't get controversial.

Some topics should be off limits until you get to know each other better. If she suddenly stops talking, you may have hit on a taboo topic. Here are some things not to talk about on your first date:

- **Sex.** Yeah, that's not a good way to kick off the date. It may be what you are thinking about, but you don't need to let her know that. Talking about sex – including anything in your past, fantasies, porn sites, etc. – is most likely going to come across as threatening to your date.
- **Your exes.** While exes can sometimes accidentally pop up in conversations, try not to let that happen, and if it does, don't dwell there.
- **Politics.** While current events can be good conversation starters, you need to be careful about getting into controversial topics – especially if you disagree on the topic. You most likely won't change each other's minds when it comes to beliefs, but you may very well ruin your date.
- **Religion.** This one is not always a faux pas. If you met at a church or religious event, then there's a strong likelihood that you share at least some of the same beliefs. But it can also be a big turnoff for your date depending on his or her beliefs.

Flirting Fun

While small talk is great and all, remember you are on a date and you should have fun. If you are having fun, then flirting can make it even better – if done appropriately.

The heart of flirting is simply showing interest. You are flirting because you are interested in knowing her a little better. And by flirting, you are showing your date you are interested in her. Plus, to be frank, it can be a big turn on.

Let's talk about how to flirt:

- **Make eye contact.** We've talked about this throughout the book, but there's a reason eye contact is so important. Looking someone directly in the eye is very enthralling. You are showing your date that you are captivated by her.
- **Smile.** Smiling is very attractive and engaging. Just be careful and don't be insincere when you smile. An insincere smile is a smirk, and it's a very unpleasant expression.
- **Pay attention.** Don't check your phone. Don't let your mind wander off. Ask questions related to what she says so she knows you're paying attention.
- **Use your whole body.** In addition to making eye contact, lean forward, smile, untense your hands and arms. Try to let your body language show you are relaxed.
- **Focus on your date, not yourself.** Try not to overpower the conversation.
- **Don't overstep.** There's a big difference between brushing your date's arm and grabbing her butt. Or saying that she has a beautiful smile verses that she has a smoking hot body. Go slow and practice subtlety.
- **Don't be afraid.** You may feel uncomfortable flirting, and that's OK. It's better to be sincere than too slick.

Watch her nonverbal cues:

When women are feeling attracted to a man, one of the first things they do is toss or sweep their hair back. Now, don't take that as the end-all response, but it's one that is commonly subconsciously practiced.

Here are some other positive nonverbal cues to watch for in your date:

- **Good eye contact.**
- **Leaning forward.** Making the area between you two a little cozier signals interest.
- **Relaxed posture.** If she is sitting or standing comfortably, chances are she feels comfortable with you.
- **Touching.** In a gentle, friendly way (not sexual).
- **Nodding.** – But not too much. A little is good. Too much means she's not really paying attention.
- **Copying your cues, or mirroring.** If her body is doing things similar to yours – leaning in, legs crossed like yours, etc., she is subconsciously in sync with you.

Here are a few negative cues:

- **Open mouth.** If she looks like she's constantly ready to speak but can't, you are probably talking too much.
- **Hands over mouth.** She is probably trying not to say something negative.
- **Arms crossed.** This can indicate a barrier between you, but it can also just mean she's cold.
- **Yawning.** It could be that she's bored, or it could just be that she's honestly tired. Either way, when you start to see yawning, it's time to call it a night.

Chapter 11: Enjoying Your Date

Remember, your date doesn't have to be life changing, but it should be fun. For that to happen, you need to create an environment that allows both you and your date to relax and get to know each other.

Remember, a date has a beginning, a middle, and an end, so pace yourself. Your date doesn't have to fall in love with you in the first few minutes, and you don't have to love her either. Keep reminding yourself that your goal is simply to get to know one another better.

By this point, you should have already figured out where you are going on your date. Most likely, food will be involved at some point.

Here are a few tips when it comes to eating:

- Don't order finger foods, like sandwiches, tacos, or even burgers. They can easily fall apart and make a big mess.
- Pizza often has long gooey cheese. And spaghetti? Forget about it.
- Be careful about drinking alcohol. Moderation is the key, and this can be difficult when you're nervous. Nerves actually increase the effect of alcohol, so you feel drunk faster. Too much alcohol makes it hard to focus or use good judgment. And obviously, you don't want to risk drinking and driving.
- Tip well. Women like men who show generosity. Treat your wait staff politely as well - but don't flirt.
- Chew with your mouth closed. Seems obvious, but you'd be surprised.
- Use your napkin (but don't tuck it in your shirt).
- Practice your manners. At the very least, open and hold the door for her. Holding her chair while she sits can also earn you bonus points in many situations.

Silence is OK

Even the best conversations can have a lull, so don't panic if the conversation hits a slow point. Everybody worries about not having anything to say, but if you can, remind yourself you are in charge. Ask questions.

When Dates Go Awry

No matter how much planning goes into it, there's no way to ensure that your date will go flawlessly. The key is to prepare for the worst so you can keep from panicking when those misfortunes comes your way.

Rule number one is that no matter what the problem is, tell her immediately. Your date is going to know that something is wrong and think it has to do with her. It's better just to confess and, if possible, even have a laugh.

Here are a few scenarios and solutions:

1. You pants or shirt split. If you have a jacket or sweater, wrap it around your waist. Or see if your waiter has a safety pin.

2. You forgot your wallet. At this point, your only option is to let the restaurant or your date know, and see if they can help you. (This is another good reason to select a restaurant that you are familiar with and where the staff hopefully at least recognize you.

3. You get carded and don't have your identification with you. If you can't get in, you can't get in. Come up with a plan B.

4. You get sick. Be honest. Tell your date you aren't feeling well and need to run to the rest room. If you don't think you can make it, you need to ask your date for help.

5. You pass gas. Apologize once, then open a window. Don't make a joke about it (unless she does first).

6. You run across your angry ex. Keep calm. Let your ex make a fool of herself, but don't join her.

7. Your car breaks down. Call for a tow truck, then try to get a ride to where your date was supposed to be. If the tow truck is going to take too long, call for a cab or Uber to take your date home. This is a time when that extra cash you took out beforehand could come in handy.

If something negative happens with your date -- like her pants split, or she trips and falls, or she forgets her I.D., don't get angry and don't laugh (unless she does first). Just let her know it's OK and you're sorry that it happened.

Picking up the Check

If you asked her out, you should pick up the tab - or at least try to. If she insists, then you can either let her pay for part of it, tell her she can pay the tip, or let her pay for coffee (or whatever you go to do next). Or, if things are going well, tell her she can pay next time. (That way you've already planted the idea of the next date in her brain.)

By paying for the date you are showing:

- You aren't cheep
- You have class.
- You are investing in the relationship, even if it's just one date.

Just know that paying does not mean that she owes you:

- Another date
- A kiss
- Sex.
- Anything else.

Ending the Date

Telling when the date has ended isn't always as simple as it seems it should be. There are definitely cues – your table is cleared off, the music has stopped, the sun has come up.

When you are on a good date and enjoying good company, your brain releases a chemical called *phenylethylamine* (PEA), which is what creates that euphoric tingling sensation. Your brain may also be releasing other natural uppers like dopamine and norepinephrine. These chemicals create a natural high, which is what causes the romantic desire to stay awake and talk into the wee hours of the morning.

However, these chemicals in your brain fade.

Even if you're having a wonderful time on that first date, it's smarter to pace yourself in the long run. Leave her wanting more as opposed to almost giving her too much. If your date went well, you want it to be the beginning of a relationship, not the end of one night you will always remember.

We'll be diving into more details of various dating outcomes, but for now, keep these general rules in mind on how to end your date with tact.

For Good Dates

If you've had a good time on your date and would like to see her again, bring up the idea of a second date before your first one ends. You don't have to schedule it yet, but you can bring it up. Then tell her you will call her.

As an important side note, don't tell her you will call her if you have no intentions of doing so.

For OK Dates

Sometimes it's hard to tell if a date went well or not. You may think it went great at the time, but looking back, realize that maybe you're not interested. Or maybe you thought it went bad, but looking back you realize you'd like to see her again.

You don't have bring up a second date, yet. Or, if you bring it up and she says she'll think about it, just smile and respond "great." Then go home and get on with life. If she calls, she calls. But don't let it stop you if she doesn't.

If you're not sure how you feel about your date, give yourself a week or so to figure it out.

At the end of the date, you certainly don't want to have sex.

For Horrible Dates

If you are just ready for the date to end and never see her again, do not say you'll call. If she brings up the idea of a second date and you have no interest, it's best to be politely honest. Say something like

"I'm glad we did this tonight, and let's just wait and see what happens." That's not really direct, but it's not lying either.

To Kiss or Not to Kiss

This is always a tricky question at the end of your first date. (Note, sex should not be an option yet, so don't think about going there.)

If you want to kiss her, start off by trying to read her body language. If she extends her hand, that probably means that she doesn't want a kiss. It's not always a brush off. It can just be her being awkward. If you want more, hold her extended hand then move in for a hug instead.

Hugs are a little more intimate, without going over the top. It's a pretty safe option. If your date moves in and hugs you close – and you enjoy it – you can either give her a quick kiss on her head or cheek, or if you're really feeling brave, move in for a kiss.

The next step is a quick kiss. In some cultures, this is just a normal greeting, so there shouldn't be a ton of pressure on you. A quick peck on the cheek is usually a nice way to safely say goodnight without being rejected.

A serious kiss is the big one. This is a kiss of intention and takes on a more sexual than friendly tone. It's one of the best indicators that your date wants to see you again. But, unless you know there's a strong vibe for a serious kiss, start with the hug and quick kiss. She may even move on to the serious kiss so you don't have to.

Here are some other signs that indicate she's wanting a goodnight kiss:

- She is facing you and is relaxed with her arms down.
- Her head is tilted upward.
- She's gazing in your eyes.
- Her lips are parted and relaxed.
- She doesn't say anything that indicates she's ready to end the date.

On the other hand, if she is not interested, she will give you signs as well:

- Her jaw is clamped shut.
- She avoids eye contact.
- Her chin is tucked down towards her chest.
- She holds out her hand to shake it. (Again, that could just be her nerves.)

Making out is the last step before sex. Sometimes it leads to sex - but on your first date, I highly recommend not going there. This consists of lots of serious kisses, hands, bodies pressed together, etc. If you don't want to see her again, don't go there.

Men often mistakenly think that serious kissing naturally leads to sex. Women, on the other hand, are often satisfied with kissing alone. Women could kiss all night and be happy. Men often feel cheated if it doesn't end in sex. Women often are more turned on by a guy who will stop before having sex on the first date.

That said, having sex on the first date really is not a great idea. You are just now getting to know each other. Again, it's better to leave her wanting more and to take things slower if you are really interested in each other. Sex often means more to women than it does to men. While it may not be a big deal to you, she may already be thinking about a wedding dress. It's best to slow down and make sure you're on the same page.

Post-Date Perspective

Every date you go on – good or bad – has a time where you (and your date) relive the moments from your date in your mind. Be warned that your memory is going to be skewed and can be misleading. You are going to exaggerate both the good and the bad of your date. Just try to keep the date in perspective. Try to remember, even with a great date, it's still just a date. If you are already convinced it's your happily-ever-after, you may be in for a pretty heavy heartbreak.

Once you get home, take about 10 minutes and repeat the relaxation techniques you did before the date. If you are having difficulty sleeping, write down your thoughts in a notebook by your bed so you have them on paper, then try to let them go so you can sleep.

Chapter 12: Bad Dates

First, it's just a fact of life that not everyone is going to like you. So if your date doesn't like you, don't act like it's the end of the world. It may feel kind of crummy knowing your date doesn't like you enough to go out again, but it's just one person's opinion.

In fact, a bad date can actually be a good thing because it gives you the chance to take a deeper look at yourself, your hopes, your signals, who you pick to date, how you act on a date, how relaxed you are on a date, and how well you communicate the real you. The key is to not take it all too personally, and certainly don't let it keep you from trying again.

There are some signals that a date isn't going well, but these can also be misread. A yawn may not mean she's bored, just that it's been a tiring day. If she's checking her watch it may just be a habit. Lack of eye contact may be more that she's shy than that she doesn't like you.

Are You Just Being Paranoid?

If you sense that your date is not having a good time, you may wonder if you're reading things right or if you're just being paranoid. After all, a date can be a pretty vulnerable experience. It's normal to feel a little nervous or insecure.

Before you write the date off as a "no go," ask yourself a few questions:

- Am I looking for hidden meanings in everything she says?
- Am I preoccupied with how I sound or come across?
- Has anyone ever said I'm oversensitive?

- Has anyone ever said I'm paranoid?

If any or most of these are the case, you may actually want to rethink whether you are ready to date at all.

Reading the Signs

It's usually fairly easy to tell when someone can't stand you. They shoot you dirty looks, scowl, sneer, jeer, or even cuss you out. But a not-so-great date may be harder to read. Often, what happens is a slow disconnect - and you grow further apart as the night wears on.

Here are a few warning signs that the date is not going well:

- **She avoids eye contact.** She may be shy, but if she's feeling comfortable, she should begin to make eye contact as the date progresses. Or if she started off strong in the eye contact area but wanes as the evening goes along, she's probably feeling disconnected.
- **She is sullen or unresponsive.** If she's not talking, it could be because you are monopolizing the conversation or asking too many personal questions. But if you are asking questions and only getting "yeah" or "no" or "don't know," there's a good chance she's not interested.
- **She is monopolizing the conversation.** If she is only talking about herself and showing no sign of interest in you, either she is not interested in getting to know you, or she's just preoccupied with herself – which may be a warning sign for you.
- **She doesn't share your humor.** If you find yourself laughing alone, explaining stories, or just having a hard time getting in sync, it's either that she doesn't like you or she just doesn't get you.

- **Body language indicates she's not interested.** If she looks like she's trying to figure out a way to escape the whole date, then chances are she is.
- **She seems sad or unhappy.** If your date is obviously emotional or sad and it doesn't get better, it's probably not a good sign. It may simply be that she's not emotionally ready to date yet.

One of the worst things you can do if you feel the date is heading south is to panic, get nervous, get quiet, or overreact. That's only going to make the situation worse.

If you sense things aren't going well, the best – and hardest - thing to do is bring it up. It's better to know what your date is feeling than to struggle and stress over it. Here are some examples of things you could say:

- I'm concerned you're not enjoying our date. Am I right?
- Please be honest. Are you having fun?
- Have I said or done or something to offend you?
- It seems like we're not quite clicking. Am I right?

It's not always fun to hear the truth; but most of the time, if given the opportunity to be honest, women will be polite about it. You don't need or want to date someone who isn't interested in you. You don't want to have to try to convince someone to date you. Sometimes a date is just not a good match, so just accept it and try again with someone new. Try not to take it too personally.

If you find out your date isn't interested in you or isn't have a good time, you need to just listen respectfully and without getting defensive, smile, and make an exit as soon as you can. There's no need to keep a bad date going.

Just say something like "You don't seem to be having a good time. Why don't we just call it a night? We can just use this as a learning experience." Or the age-old "I think we should just be friends." That's much better than pretending all is great while wishing the date could just end.

Some couples don't have chemistry. It's nothing personal. While some couples grow to love each other, having chemistry up front really is helpful because it motivates you to keep seeing each other. That being said, if you do find yourself enjoying your date's company but you don't necessarily find yourself attracted to her, you might not want to call it quits until at least another date or two.

Tuition for Dating 101

You may feel pretty crummy if your date turns out to be a disaster. Try to remind yourself once again that it's just one date. Make it a learning experience.

While the date is fresh on your mind, jot down things you remember. Start by writing down the date, your date's name, how you met, where you went on your date, and how you'd rate your date on a scale from 1 to 10. Next, you might be able to figure out where things went wrong by answering the following questions:

1. What went well on your date? What was positive?
2. What went wrong? What disappointed you?
3. What were your expectations before the date?
4. Why do you think you had those expectations? Were they based on a prior experience?
5. If you have been on prior dates, what patterns do you see when you compare this one with those?
6. How are you feeling now?

7. What do you want to do next? (Try again? Call a friend? Take a break from dating?)
8. What do you think you could do differently on your next date that would help?
9. How comfortable were you on your date?

By answering these questions after every not-so-great date, it can help you learn from your dates rather than wallow in self-pity.

What if You Hate Your Date?

In some cases, your date may have a great time and you may have a miserable time. Remember, again, it's just one date. Use it to learn about yourself and what you like – or in this case, dislike – about a date.

The whole point of dating, remember, is to get to know someone better. You aren't going to like everyone, and not everyone will like you. That's human nature. However, you can be kind when you realize your date is not the right one for you.

Don't Cut it Short

As tempting as it may be to ditch your annoying date or at least tell her it was a mistake, don't. You can find ways to call it a night early without leaving her eating alone.

If your date is having a good time but you are not, here are some ideas to try. They can help get you through the evening and allow you more opportunity to find out some interesting things about your date and yourself.

If you're not having a good time but your date is, give these strategies a try.

1. Come up with three qualities you like about your date. It's sometimes easy to focus on the negative and forget the positive. Come up with three things – even if they're small. Do you like her hair? Her laugh?
2. Practice listening. Even if you're miserable because she won't stop talking, this is a good time to practice listening for future dates. Plus, you might actually find something she says interesting.
3. Chill and enjoy your surroundings. The food, the atmosphere, the sunshine – focus on the things around you and try to find something about them that you enjoy. Shift your focus away from your lousy date and find something enjoyable in the situation.

Be polite

Your date may not go as you had hoped, but don't let that prevent you from using good manners.

1. It's already been said in this chapter, but don't ditch your date. Don't fake a headache, hide in the restroom, or take off when she's not looking
2. Keep talking. Don't sit quietly and sulk. Do your best to keep the conversations going.
3. Look her in the eye. You don't need to flirt, but you don't want to stare at the ceiling either.
4. Pay attention. Don't stop listening to her just because things aren't going as you'd hoped.
5. Be kind. Don't be rude. Don't roll your eyes, or shake your head, because you're annoyed.
6. Make sure your date makes it home safely. If you drove her there, drive her home. If she met you somewhere, walk her back to her car. Or share a ride.

7. Obey the golden rule. Treat your date as you'd want to be treated.

Be Cautiously Honest

If you know it's not going to work out with your date, you may want to be honest. But if you do so, do it tactfully. Imagine yourself in your date's place.

Here are some examples of things you can say:

- Wow, it's getting late and I've got an early day tomorrow.
- Sorry I keep yawning. It's been a long day.
- You've led such a different life than I have.
- Your picture doesn't do you justice.
- You are so full of energy!
- Tonight's sure been an experience.

One time that you need to be honest is if she asks if you will call her, or if she can call you. It's not fair to leave her waiting by the phone if you really have no intention of calling. So don't say you will call if you don't plan to. Here are a few responses you could use instead:

- I had fun tonight, but I don't believe it's going to work out for us.
- I really see you more as a friend.
- We are just too different.

Or you can make up something like, "My schedule is really busy the next few months."

Dealing with Hurt Feelings

Just because you don't find a connection with your date doesn't mean you have to be cruel. Don't string your date along by pretending you like her if you don't. In the long run, it's really meaner to string your date along than to be honest.

You don't need to feel guilty about being honest as long as you've been a gentleman. You asked her out based on an assumption that you would connect. But, you didn't.
If your date is upset:

- Recognize that she has the right to feel upset. Don't get defensive or pretend all is good if she lashes out at you.
- Don't try to change her feelings.
- Tell her you're sorry that she feels hurt, but don't apologize for not feeling connected to her. You didn't do anything wrong.
- Let go and move on.

Learn from the Experience

The best thing you can do with a bad date is use it to determine specifically what went wrong. When you get home and the date is still fresh in your mind, write down in your dating notebook today's date, your date's name, and score the overall date on a scale from 1 to 10.

Next, make two columns: "What I originally liked about her," and "What I ended up not liking about her." Then be honest and detailed. Write down everything you can think of.

What if You Both Don't Like Each Other?

Sometimes bad dates just happen. It's not necessarily anyone's fault.

After having a really good date, having a really bad date where neither party is enjoying themselves is actually the next best scenario. That way, neither of you gets your feeling hurt. It's much better than one person having a good time and the other having a bad time. It's easy to wish each other the best and move on

Facing Facts

As long as this isn't a completely blind date where you've had no interaction with each other before, you probably both had some positive feelings towards each other before the date took place. However, after the actual date got started, that attraction began to be tested. Deciding whether you like someone or not sometimes takes a little time.

From the moment you first meet, your brain starts recording and processing everything that you and your date do or say. It usually takes a little bit for your brain to realize that things aren't meshing between you. Before you decide your date is a total waste, check a few things:

- **Are you feeling relaxed or anxious?** Again, some nerves are normal, but if you are so tense that your true personality can't show, your date may actually dislike your anxiousness, not your personality. Remember, if you're too tense, breathe.
- **Does your date seem relaxed?** Again, her personality may not be really shining through if she's a bundle of nerves. Try to make your date feel more comfortable by initiating

conversation and being friendly. Try not to judge too harshly until she seems a little more relaxed.
- **Did your date say something that bothered you?** One careless remark can blow a whole date. Try to remember that one dumb comment doesn't necessarily reflect her entire personality. If something she says really seems inappropriate, it's OK to tell her that.
- **Are you judging too harshly?** Don't let small things completely turn you off. You are in a more anxious state and small things might irk you more at the moment than they normally would.

That being said, there are times when your date does something that completely turns you off and offends you. For example, maybe she makes a racist remark. Or if it's a guy, maybe he cops a feel on his date. In those cases, it's ok just to say you can tell things aren't going to work out.

Be Honest

If you are unhappy on your date, and you sense your date is too, here's what to do:

- Trust your gut.
- Ask. "I get the feeling we aren't really connecting. Is that accurate?"
- Be honest. If your date asks what's wrong, it's ok to say that things aren't going as well as you'd hoped, then ask if your date feels the same way.

If both of you confess that you're not really enjoying the date, it's OK to call it a night. But do it with class.

- I'm ready to call it a night. Is that OK with you?

- Thank you for sharing your evening with me. Do you need a ride home?
- I'm sorry things didn't work out.
- Let's consider this a learning experience.

Reviewing the Date

A single bad date doesn't really mean much. If it's a common theme, however, there may be more to the story.

When you get home and the date is still fresh in your mind, pull out your dating notebook. Answer the following questions:

- What qualities does your ideal date need to have?
- What qualifies should your ideal date not have?
- What went wrong with this date?
- What went wrong with your other bad dates?
- Are there any common threads between your bad dates?

Look over your lists and see if there are similarities between what went wrong with your date(s) and the "my date must not have these qualities" lists.

For example, if your ideal date must not be boring, loud, and obese, and your date was boring, loud, and thin, then perhaps you only focused on your date's exterior before the date.

Your Next Step

If you have a bad date, don't let it stop you from trying again. Problem solving is a much better response than giving up. Figure out what went wrong then try to correct the course on your next date.

That being said, don't rush into another date with just anybody without using your failed date as guide.

Part 3: The Second Date and Beyond

Chapter 13: The Second Date

So, you got the stressful first date out of the way and it was successful. N,ow it's time for date number two. You're a little more comfortable but it's still kind of stressful and exciting. The key is to try to relax a bit, keep your expectations under control, and keep the new relationship moving forward.

Is This Really Your Second Date, or Your First?

For this to be considered your second date, you should have gone through at least some of the steps we talked about in earlier chapters where you actually asked her out, planned the date ahead of time, showered before you met up with her, spent two or three hours together, etc. If it was a spontaneous "let's go get coffee after class," that may not have been a full-blown date, making this your first date.

It's not necessarily a big deal, except when we refer to second dates. If your first get together was a mini date – a spontaneous get together – the next time you go out is actually your first official date. If that's the case, you may want to go back and read through all the first date-related content first.. If it's all just a bunch of spontaneous get togethers, you're just "hanging out", not dating. There's a difference.

Anatomy of a true second date

A second date means you've already made it past all the stressors of the first date, but you're not in a relationship yet. Your first date was all about mystery and fantasy – looking and acting your best. For the second date, you start to delve into reality. You both relax a little more and you get to know the realistic versions of each other better.

Keep in mind that a second date is only a second date. You are not yet in a relationship. It is a time to continue determining if you are compatible and if you want to keep moving forward. It is a chance to get to know each other better. Your "real" personalities start to show a little more – which is both good and bad.

A second date consists of more:

- **Communicating.** You'll start to dig a little deeper when talking with each other, learning more about each other's histories, families, work, etc. Nothing super sensitive, but more personal than talking about the weather.
- **Testing for compatibility.** You start to focus less on making a good impression to learning more about your date and if she might be a good match.
- **Searching for shared interests.** You start to find out more about what your date likes and doesn't like.
- **Flirting.**
- **Prolonged eye contact.** (Which goes along with flirting)

Good Second Date Options

The goal of a second date is to get a deeper glimpse into each other and be a little more intimate, so where you go for your second date should allow for those types of things.

Some good options include:

- A quiet restaurant
- A museum
- A park

Bad options include:

- A noisy bar
- A movie
- Your place (or hers)

What to Expect

Keep in mind that what happens after your first date and before the second will effect date number two. If you were lusting all over each other during the first date and have been talking on the phone every day since, your second date is going to be much different than if you waited two weeks to call after your first date.

If it has been more than two weeks since your first date, and especially if you haven't been talking to each other regularly, your second date is going to feel a lot more like a first date.

Your expectations are going to be different for your second date than they were for the first one, but you need to keep them in check. If you had an incredible first date, your expectations for date number two may be too high and you may be disappointed. Same goes for having really low expectations. If possible, try to approach your second date without having huge expectations either way.

Of course, it's not possible to completely eliminate your expectations. It's easy to get stressed out if your second date doesn't measure up to your high expectations. Don't dwell on that thought. It will prevent you from having fun, which will prevent your date from having fun.

If you start to feel tense or stressed during the date, breathe. Then take a moment to think about these things:

- What is bothering you? Are you blaming your date for your unrealistic expectations? Are you remembering past negative experiences?
- Are you afraid of getting too close to your date? Second dates involve revealing more intimate things about your life, and maybe that scares you more than you thought it would.
- Are you falling into old patterns? Sometimes we do negative things because we get scared.

Negative Dating Patterns

Sometimes people fall into the same old patterns in relationships. Some fall for a date way to quickly, then lose interest just as quickly. Some move way to quickly – professing their love too soon – and scare their dates away. Watch for patterns and consciously work toward changing them.

Everyone has dating patterns. Some are just more negative than others. If you know you have some negative patterns and want to change them, follow these steps:

- **Identify your behavior.** As soon as you feel a "Oops... I did it again" moment, stop and think about why.
- **Define your behavior.** Come up with a mental description of your behavior. "When I get nervous, I tend to get defensive."
- **Pinpoint what set you off this time.**
- **File it away until you're alone.** If something sets you off during your date, make a mental note to revisit it later, then move on until after the date.

Solving the First 15 Minute Dilemmas

Second dates don't require as much planning as first dates. That said, there is more at risk, so you do want to put some thought into it so you can relax and enjoy. You want to prepare to solve any dilemmas you will face in the first 15 minutes of your date.

Here are some examples:

- Should you kiss your date when you first meet? A kiss on the cheek is OK (if you've already done this). Don't kiss her on the lips.
- Should you hold her hand? Not yet.
- Should you talk about your last date together? That's fine, and it's good to bring up something you talked about before.
- Should you go somewhere different from your first date? Yes.
- Do I have to spend a lot? No. If you don't have a lot to spend, choose something inexpensive or free, like a walk in the park.

Diving Deeper

Conversations on a second date are less superficial than the first date. You learned a little about each other on the first date, and now you can build on that foundation. You don't want to share all your problems or issues, but it's OK to let your date know you're not perfect.

To learn more about your date – warts and all – you have to be open to sharing more about yourself as well. Second date conversation should be a good give and take between both of you.

Being aware of your own personality before the date can help. Are you quiet and reserved? A type A who tends to control conversations? Do you like to debate about politics, etc.? Being aware of these kinds of things can help you tone it down, or amp it up, depending on the situation.

Here are some things to watch out for:

- If it seems you know everything about your date but she knows nothing about you, it's time to open up.
- Are you dominating the conversation? Let her talk.
- If all you're doing is entertaining, tone it down and focus on learning more about your date.
- If all you're doing is talking about work, try to get a little more personal.
- If your date seems uncomfortable when you ask her more personal questions, back off.

In some cases, second date conversation can be like pulling teeth. If you are running out of things to talk about, stop and reflect. If she talked a lot on the first date but is quiet now, you may just want to ask. "We had a great time on our first date. Is something wrong?" If she says no and the pace continues to lull, then two dates may be enough.

Sharing More

The more dates you go on with the same person, the deeper the conversation should get. What information you should share and when you should share it depends on your comfort level as well as your dates. If your date is open and accepting, you will probably feel more comfortable sharing more. If your date is more reserved, you probably will feel less comfortable sharing.

Some people are fine with sharing some areas of their lives, but not others. Again, you're trying to find compatibility. So share what you're comfortable sharing to someone you don't know all that well, and save the rest for later. In fact, it's best not to air all your dirty laundry in the beginning. In fact, you can even plan ahead and determine what you do or don't want to let your date know about you yet.

Here are some good starting points:

- **Start with some of your life facts.** Where you're from, where you went to school, your hobbies, your work, and your siblings.
- **Share a few feelings.** Things you like or don't like. Some small worries that you have.

As you share, stay positive and realistic. Don't brag, but don't put yourself down either.

Remember the following:

- **You don't really know each other.** Don't divulge something you'll regret later.
- **Don't share information to try to guilt your date into staying.** Divulging your innermost secrets as a way to make them feel sorry for you or worry about dumping you is not a healthy practice.
- **Don't do all the divulging.** If you are sharing every intimate secret and she won't even tell you her favorite movie, the conversation is not balanced. Also, make sure you don't hog the conversation.

As you continue to date and really get to know each other, your conversations and actions should change significantly. You don't want to keep a secret that if later found out would completely destroy your relationship. But you also don't need to share that secret too early for there to be a context for understanding.

What to Share - and When:

Within the first three or four dates:

- Share anything that can affect long-term prospects that more than two people already know. If more than two people know about it, it's really not a secret. Keeping a big secret from the start adds pressure and nervousness, and usually only gets worse with time. For example, if you have a child, if you've been in jail, or if you've been married before.
- If you've mislead your date by saying you enjoy doing something that you really don't, you need to let her know fairly early on. So, for example, if you said you were a big football fan and you're not, you need to fess up.

Before Having Sex:

These topics really need to be talked about when you are not in the heat of passion. Do it beforehand.

- **Contraception.** What kind? Who is in charge?
- **Condoms.** Again, whose responsibility?
- **STDs** – past or present.
- **History of sexual abuse if it effects your current sexual relationship.**
- **Past relationships.** If it's something that's going to impact your current relationship.
- **If you are a virgin.**
- **If you aren't ready yet.** Or if want to wait until you get married.

Again, these are reasons to wait to have sex until you are really comfortable with one another emotionally.

Things to Tell if Asked

You may not want to offer up this type of information unless asked, but once asked, it's OK to divulge –if you're comfortable. Questions about past relationships, for example. If you just totally refuse to answer, it will make you look like you're hiding something. So if you're comfortable, tell what you're comfortable with, but don't go into a ton of detail. That said, you don't have to answer anything unless you really want to.

Sharing Feelings

Creating guidelines for sharing feelings is not black and white. In the early stages of dating, especially, everything is still a bit delicate.

A smart idea is to set some ground rules together to figure out what you both want and need. This takes trust; and trust takes time.

Here are some guidelines:

- **Err on the side of caution.** Don't divulge your feelings if you aren't comfortable, and don't go overboard. Don't profess your undying love on the first few dates.
- **Live with your feelings before expressing them.** Make sure that what you think you're feeling is true for more than just the moment. If someone cuts you off when you're driving and it makes you angry, are you still going to be angry in an hour? If not, then don't give him the bird. (Don't do that anyway, especially in front of your date!)
- **Think before you speak.** You need to put your emotions in perspective before you profess them. Are you really feeling love, or are you actually feeling thankful – or horny?

- **Is what you're feeling realistic?** You may feel like you're madly in love and ready to spend the rest of your life with this woman, but if it's only your first date, is that accurate?

Keeping Your Mouth Shut

You don't want to lie, but sometimes it's better to just keep your mouth shut. If you really feel compelled to tell your date something controversial, make a quick trip to the bathroom. Write the thing down, then think about why you feel the need to fess up. Is it to make yourself feel better? Because you're scared and trying to sabotage the relationship? If all you can come up with is "I just want to be honest," keep your mouth shut.

Here are some examples of things not to talk about:

- Details of past relationships
- If you've ever cheated
- Your bank account
- Gossip
- Your friends' feelings about your date
- Your bigotry

For the most part, talking about past relationships is just a bad idea – period. They are "past" relationships for a reason. When it comes to past relationships, especially past sexual experiences - don't ask, don't tell. They are over with and nothing good can come from talking about them.

Questions to Ask or Avoid

In addition to knowing what to tell, you need to know what is OK to ask. Asking questions makes your date feel important. Good questions draw your date out without making her uncomfortable. Keep these tips in mind:

- **Ask about a variety of things.** Topics can range from current events, to pop culture, to work. Just try not to focus on one topic, especially things like exes.
- **Don't think too far ahead.** If you're worried about what to ask next, you won't be able to listen to what your date is saying.
- **Don't ask aggressive questions.**
- **Don't pound your date with too many questions.**

When to Say Those Three Words

Finally, before you say "I love you," keep these things in mind:

- Wait at least three months if possible, even if you feel it on that first date.
- Don't say "I love you, too" if your date says it first and you aren't ready.
- Don't wait for your date to say it first. If you really feel it and you've waited a while to say it, take the plunge.
- Remember that "love" may not mean the same to you as it does to her. You may equate "love" to marriage. She may use "love" in everyday life with her friends.
- Realize that "love" usually implies you are ready to be monogamous.
- The term "love" is not synonymous with "I want to have sex."

Chapter 14: The Stages of Dating

For a relationship to survive, you both need to be on the same page. You may think you're in a casual relationship while she thinks you're serious. This, obviously, can cause issues.

Let's look at the differences:

Casual Dating:

If you are casually dating, neither of you considers the relationship as being too serious. Reasons for casual dating may mean:

- You're free to see other people.
- You live far away and only get to see each other occasionally.
- You are only in the area for a temporary amount of time, like for a business trip, vacation, etc.
- You're not looking for a commitment.

Casual dating has its perks. It allows both of you to get to know each other without the pressure of exclusivity. It also lets you compare your date with other potential partners.

Serious Dating

When dating seriously:

- You are seeing each other exclusively
- You see each other at least once a week.
- You live in the same area.
- You may or may not be having sex.

Heavy Dating

This is the most serious form of dating. By the time you reach heavy dating:

- You've both verbally agreed to being mutually exclusive.
- You see each other several times a week.
- You usually spend your weekends together.
- You live in the same community.

How Relationships Progress

If you've made it successfully past your second date, you are probably beyond the "just friends" stage, but you're not really yet in a relationship. This is an exciting, scary, mysterious place to be. It's best to go slowly, keep things in perspective, and stay in the moment. Don't think too far ahead and don't dwell on the past.

Just as you're getting comfortable, understand your date may begin planning ahead. Playing dumb and/or oblivious will cost you more than it's worth in the long run.

Let's take a look at how most dating relationships progress.

Stage 1 (from first date to one month): You are both just getting interested in each other, and there's a spark. You are still putting your best self forward – dressing nicely, showering before each date, and so on.

Stage 2 (1 to 3 months): You are moving forward, getting to know each other better. You're comfortable enough around each other to relax a bit more, choosing to not only wear your best outfits, for example.

Stage 3 (3 to 6 months): Things are heating up, both physically and emotionally. You like each other and feel comfortable enough to just hang out.

Stage 4 (6 to 9 months): You are in a *real* relationship. You may not have said the "L" word yet, but you feel it. You've gotten to know and accept each other's flaws.

Sex and Dating

Sex is about more than just being physically intimate. It's also about being emotionally intimate, which is why I keep stressing the need to hold off on having sex until you are further along in the relationship. Having sex only for the physical aspects often leads to hurt and feeling alone.

When is the right time to have sex? Ideally, you need to wait until you know and trust each other, and you both want to have sex because you like each other, not to yield power over the other person.

Beyond that, it's best to have done the following things first :
1. Talk about it. Before you have sex, find out what you each think about sex, what it means to you, and what it means for the relationship. If you're not ready to talk about sex, you really aren't ready to have sex.
2. 2You have passionate feelings for this person, not just sexual feelings. There's a difference between eating because you're starving and eating because you are enjoying the meal. The same holds true for sex.
3. You've had at least three dates, preferably more.
4. You love touching each other.
5. You see each other more than once a week.

6. Neither of you are having sex with anyone else.
7. You're prepared to have safe sex.
8. You both feel ready and are still enjoying each other.

"Yes" or "No"

The only reason to ever say yes to sex is because you sincerely and wholeheartedly want to have sex with the other person. You should not say yes because you are afraid to say no, because all your friends are doing it, because you don't want to lose your relationship, and so on.

That being said, if you're not ready, that's OK too. You can say no; and if she says no, don't try to convince her to change her mind. If she changes it on her own and is sure she's ready, then you can move forward.

When it's time to actually have sex, keep in mind that the first time with anyone can be a little awkward. Try not to set your expectations too high or get too low if things don't go perfectly.

Stay or Go?

As your relationship progresses, you are going to hit different stages. At that point it's time to evaluate whether you want to move forward or get out.

Early relationships tend to focus more on the fun side of dating. As you grow, however, the fun and excitement gets traded in for more depth. The following guide can help you determine whether you are staying because you really want to or if you are settling.

Answer the following questions:

- How much time do the two of you spend together?
- How much of that together time do you enjoy?
- Is your time together increasing or decreasing?
- How often do you argue or fight?
- How much do you have in common?
- Do you like to do the same things? List specifics.
- Do you like each other's friends?
- Are your religious beliefs aligned? Political beliefs?
- Do you have similar tastes in music? Movies?
- Do you have similar life goals?
- Are you in compatible stages of life?
- Do you both want the same things from your relationship?
- Do you have similar beliefs about spending money and time?
- Are you both comfortable talking about feelings? Friends? Family? Etc.?
- Do you have similar family backgrounds?
- Do you have similar views on smoking, alcohol, etc.?
- Do you have fun together?
- Do you share similar senses of humor?
- Are you both neat freaks? Or both messy?
- How well do you listen to each other?
- How well do you negotiate or compromise?
- Are you afraid to get angry for fear of making her angry?
- Are either or both of you jealous?
- Are you possessive?
- Are you able to move past problems?

When figuring out and tallying up the answers to these questions, you are hoping to land on the middle to positive side of things. If your answers are mostly negative, you may need to consider whether this is really a healthy relationship or not.

On the one hand, don't settle for a relationship that you're not happy in just because you don't want to be alone. On the other hand, don't end a good relationship just because it's not perfect.

Chapter 15: Moving Forward…Slowly

When you are in the early stages of dating and things are going well, it's tempting to want to move forward quickly. But remember, those experiences you are longing for will still be there if you go slow, and you will be safer in the long run.

In the early stages of a relationship, a lot of it is chemistry, and it's usually more about lust than love. Lust can be a pretty powerful thing, but it can also be misleading. Those chemicals in your brain give you a natural and very real high, but eventually those chemicals fade. If you haven't built a strong foundation, then your relationship will fade as well – often catching you completely off guard.

Going slowly is about protecting yourself as well. It allows you time to figure out the following:

- Do I really like this person, or do I just like the feeling that comes from being liked?
- Do I really have feelings for this person, or do I just need someone in my life?
- Am I afraid of losing her if I don't act quickly?
- Do I really want to get to know her, or do I just want to have sex with her?

Stay in the Present

It's easy to fantasize about the future and then share those fantasies with your date. That's an easy way to scare your date off, especially if she's not thinking that seriously about your relationship or your future. It's also easy to fall back and compare your current date with your past relationships. Don't do either. Stay in the present and focus on one day at a time. That will help you build a lasting relationship because you are dealing with the real person you are dating, not your fantasy image of that person.

Ask yourself the following to determine if you may be comparing your date to a fantasy, past, or future relationship:

- Does my date remind me of a past girlfriend? Movie star? My mom?
- Do I think about how great she'd be if only ____?
- Do I obsess over what my date meant when she said or did something?
- Does it bother me if my date does something that reminds me of an old girlfriend?
- Do I know if my date feels the same way about me as I do her?

It's human nature to judge the new people in our life based on the people we've known before. The problem is if you use that past person as the basis of judging your current date. It may be that what she is doing has nothing to do with what happened when your past girlfriend did it.

Practice Patience

Lust is fast burning, but true love is slow moving. Here's the difference:

- Your likes are higher than your dislikes. You are probably keeping an unwritten checklist of things you like or dislike about your date. Things that you like are counted as compatibility points.
- Your lust for someone is based more on physical attributes than mental ones. Lust is sexual, and very powerful, but it alone won't last without love.

- Love is when you can see the other person clearly and you are still relaxed and happy. You trust the other person fully. It's acceptance, compatibility, warmth, fun, and caring despite flaws.

Sadly, relationships don't always work out. A relationship ending does not mean that it wasn't positive, productive, or valuable. And it's not necessarily anyone's fault. Even when you know it's for the best, breaking up is hard and it hurts.

Warning Signs

In many cases, people see the warning signs about their impending breakup, but put it off as long as possible for various reasons. Here are some things to watch for:

- You constantly fight over unimportant things.
- You aren't as affectionate.
- You don't like the person.
- If you were having sex before, it has stopped or significantly diminished.
- You don't hang out as much as you used to.
- You are starting to be tempted by others.
- You mentally compare your date unfavorably to others.
- You look for excuses not to see each other.
- You make a major purchase without letting her know.
- You don't return her calls or texts.

You may be convinced that a little more time and effort is what is needed to save the relationship, and that could be true. However, the first thing you need to do is determine if your partner is feeling the same way. If both of you are miserable, it's time to get counseling and/or get out of the relationship.

You also should figure out if you really want to save the relationship. To do this, write down what you want from the relationship and what you're willing to give to receive that. If there's really nothing either of you want to do to fix it, then there is really no point in continuing to try. If one of you has crossed a line, like cheating, there's no way to go back to where you once were. You can adjust to move forward, or you can get out.

Dealing with Evidence of Problems

You may very well stay in a doomed relationship much longer than you should because you didn't want to see the writing on the wall early on.

- **You may have just gone as far as you can go in your relationship.** If you are brave and want to, you can talk about the specific reasons why you are no longer interested. The cowardly option is just to quit calling or responding to her calls. Or you can make up the excuse of just being really busy. The problem is that if she is a very understanding person, she will believe you are busy and just wait for you rather than get on with her life.
- **If both of you are unhappy, it's easier to deal with.** You don't have to be brutal, but you should be honest. It's harder, however, if one person is still pretty happy, or at least content, and the other is not. If you are unhappy, it's best to be honest and ask for a break rather than just avoid the conversation. If you feel like the relationship still has a chance, it's easier to fix it later if you didn't trash it to start with. If she dumps you, you have the right to ask why – but do it honorably and without whining.
- **If you feel like your partner is drifting away, ask her about it.** "You seem to be distracted lately. If you're comfortable telling me why, maybe I can help."

Chapter 16: Breaking Up

If you tried to talk and make changes but it's still not working, it may be time to move on. Get out your notebook and make an inventory of the specifics of what is working and what's not working in your relationship. Maybe the sex is good, but you don't ever talk – or vice versa. Again, be specific. Don't just write "we can't communicate." Write down how you struggle to communicate. What are you not able to talk about? What happens when you try?

Potential Problems

1. Timing. Maybe you aren't spending as much time together as you used to or as you would like. This could be because you're tired of each other, or it could be for another reason. Maybe one of you started a new job. Maybe one of you is going to school. Unfortunately, there's often not a lot that can be done about timing. Sometimes the timing is just off, and you have to decide if it's worth waiting for it to work out or if it's better to move on.

2. Mismatched. People change, and even if you were compatible when you started dating, you may not be now. She may be wanting to settle down, you may want to travel the world. She may be thinking about having kids, while you may want to finish school. She may be a cat person, and you are a dog person. It happens.

If your main basic desires and beliefs are not compatible – things like common goals, values, and attitudes – you're going to have to continuously negotiate and compromise. This leaves you with very little reserve when a major problem arises. Opposites often attract, and sometimes they can fill the other's voids. Sometimes, however, they are just too opposite.

3. Stuck in the Past. Sometimes an old love comes back in the picture out of nowhere and throws your relationship into a tizzy. Try not to take it too personally.

4. Long Distance. Long distance relationships are really hard. Because you're not together in the day-to-day, you are often living in a fantasy world, even if you think you know each other well. By the time you actually see each other, all you can think about is getting physical, so there's not a lot of chance to get to know and experience each other's everyday quirks.

5. Physical Attraction. If your relationship is primarily physical, or if you have sex too soon, lust is in control. And as we've discussed several times already, the chemicals that cause the lustful high eventually wear off and you're stuck in reality. While it's natural to kind of lose the initial excitement that you felt on those first couple of dates, it needs to be balanced with an increase in attraction to the other person's innermost being.

On the other hand, it may be that you have a developed a great friendship, but the sexual interest just never really developed. While sexual attraction can develop in some cases, sometimes there just really is no chemistry no matter how much you'd like there to be.

6. Finances. A huge discrepancy in financial resources can cause problems, especially if you didn't know there was discrepancy from the start, or if one of your financial situations has changed. Losing a job, having major medical bills, or even inheriting a lot of money can be hard on relationships. If your partner is having money problems, do you help? What if she doesn't pay you back? Plus, there's a lot of emotional issues that come with money problems. Or if someone suddenly gains a lot of money, they have a new financial freedom that can cause problems as well.

7. Friends and family. Although you may think it doesn't matter if your friends or family like your girlfriend at first, it becomes more problematic as time goes by. Friends who once held their tongue may feel the need to tell you why she's not a good match for you.

Although you are old enough to make your own decisions, the support of your friends and family is important. They may not know what's best for you, but they also may have some valid concerns.

8. Kids. This is one of those things that is non-negotiable. If one of you wants kids and the other doesn't, it's a problem. This is something that you really should have found out before you got into the relationship. But if you didn't, or if one of you changed your mind, you've got a problem.

If you or your girlfriend already have kids, this can be a big problem in your relationship as well. It's always smart to make sure your relationship is going somewhere before introducing the kids because they become attached. If the kids really hate the idea of their parent being with someone, it's best to try to get some family counseling before calling it quits. Kids also make it harder for you to have a social life as a couple. Sometimes, it's just more than the non-parent is ready to handle.

9. Work. People, especially men, are often defined by their work. They are also taught to be providers, and so putting in long, hard hours is required. Your date may not appreciate you working so much, or vice versa, and it can be the cause of a breakup.

10. Health. Health issues cause a whole host of problems beyond health. They take up time and money, and may change your way of life. Sometimes this is just too much for the other person.

11. Substance Abuse. If you are dating someone who is addicted to drugs, alcohol, or even gambling, you need to seriously consider getting out of the relationship. Ending an addiction is a hard and a lifetime challenge. And if the other person does not want to get help, you need to leave.

12. Lost Trust. Love requires trust, and if trust has been breached, it takes a while and a lot of effort to regain it. Even then, things won't return to the way they were. If you are going to try to stay together, you both need to talk about why trust was broken in the first place. You may also want to take a break from each other so you can rethink the future of your relationship.

13. Violence. Do not stay in a violent relationship – period. If you are the violent one, admit you have a problem and get help. If you are the target of the violence, get out.

Last Ditch Efforts

When you know the relationship is getting close to ending, you may want to try a few things to repair it.

Apologize. For an apology to be beneficial, it must be specific, timely, and sincere. The bigger your mistake, the bigger the apology needs to be. If you really did something that hurt your partner, your apology should hurt you and your wallet. You're not trying to buy your way out of it, but it may help you remember the cost and not make the same mistake again.

If, on the other hand, you don't feel like you did anything wrong, don't apologize.

Take Responsibility. Sometimes you do something dumb and get caught and there's just no way to get out of it – so don't even bother.

If your partner's tears and anger have turned to indifference, it's bad. It means she's about done with you. Rather than try to make excuses, take responsibility.

Don't Share Your Fantasies. Temptations are everywhere. (Not just sexual ones.) If they weren't, it would be easier to stick to a diet.

However, if you are tempted to cheat, don't confess to your partner about your temptation. It is going to do no good to tell her you thought about cheating.

That said, if you find you are constantly fantasizing about someone else, try to figure out if it's really about the other person or if you are just wanting an excuse to break up. If it's the latter, decide if you want to fix your relationship or get out. But whatever you do, don't cheat. It's better to break up first.

Again, feeling tempted is one thing. Acting on the temptation is a whole other situation.

Don't Sabotage Your Relationship. Don't do something stupid or hurtful just to give yourself and your partner an excuse to break up. If you want out, get out. That said, don't jump ship if you don't want to, even if you are afraid your partner will.

Examples of self-sabotage include things like the following:

- Having an affair
- Acting like you don't care
- Acting violently

Self-sabotage doesn't work and only makes a bad situation worse in the end.

Take a Break. Sometimes you both just need a little space, and taking a mini break is OK if you think it may help. Breaks allow you time to think and often you also realize you miss each other. Getting some space takes you out of the day-to-day aggravation and allows you step back and get a clearer perspective. You both need to agree, however, on why you are taking a break, what the rules are (e.g., can you see other people?), and why you believe a break is a smart idea.

- If you two are normally happy but one wants a break, take a break.
- If you are crazy about each other but can't get along, take a break.
- If one of you wants to take the next step in the relationship but the other isn't ready, take a break.

Breaking Up Completely

When it's time to make a clean break, there's a right way and a wrong way to do it. Emotions are high, but ideally you can end your relationship on decent terms, at least not being hateful and nasty.

Don't Point Your Finger

The first temptation to be avoided is the need to blame somebody or something. It's really easy to want to place blame on one of you, and sometimes people even play the martyr (i.e., "It's all my fault"). The fact is, however, it's probably both of your fault, or no one's fault — however you want to say it. (There are exceptions, such as if the situation is violent or addiction is involved.) Try to say how you feel rather than pointing your finger. "I feel hurt" rather than "you hurt me."

Breakup Regrets

You probably thought that the hardest part of breaking up was getting up the courage to do it. You may have been wanting the breakup for a while, but it's still hard and it still hurts. You may even question the decision once it's made. This is normal.

Identify Patterns

If you've been through breakups before, reflect on how this relationship compared to past ones. Are there patterns? Are there things you need to try to change about yourself in the future? Talking to your partner about the patterns you see in yourself isn't very productive.

Remember the Good

Even most good things don't last forever. Just because your relationship ended doesn't mean it was all bad. Think about what you liked, what you learned, and what you apply to the future.

Spend Time Alone

Time heals all wounds, including broken hearts. Don't jump into another rebound relationship immediately. You need to deal with your current feelings and experiences, not hide from them.

After breaking up from a serious relationship, you need to avoid romance for a while. It's natural to want to jump back in and make yourself feel better. But don't. Find diversions and spend time getting healthy again. Here are some ideas:

- **Focus on friendships with other guys.** Hopefully you didn't ignore all your guy friends when you were dating. Even if you did, reach out to them and try to spend some time with them. If you don't have guy friends, try to make some.
- **Work out.** Join a gym, take up running, find a sport. Keeping physically active relieves stress and gets you looking fabulous for when it is time to reenter the dating world.
- **Find home improvement projects.** Do all those things you've been putting off, like painting the house or trimming the trees. House projects will also help you keep your home picked up rather than lazily wallowing in self-pity.
- **Find a new hobby.** Do something you've always wanted to try. Take an art class. Learn to SCUBA dive. Rebuild a car. Ride a motorcycle. Keep your mind and your body busy.
- **Dive into work.** Just make sure it doesn't become a permanent habit.

Using your rebound time wisely will reap huge benefits. You will look better, feel better, and be a better person when you are ready to get back out in the dating field.

Finally, if you're wondering how long you need to wait to recover from a breakup, there is no set in stone answer. Some suggest that you need to wait one month for every two months you were together. That may not always be necessary. However, the longer you were together, the longer you should wait. Another idea is to determine how long you think you'll need – then double that.

Self Esteem for Men

Boost your confidence and social skills, overcome low self-esteem, and transform into a fearless Alpha Male while eliminating insecurity, depression, and social anxiety.

Introduction

There is a connection between the individual and success in every area of life. There is an aspect of life that must be developed for a person to reach their highest potential. In this book, you will discover what this concept is about and how it can be utilised to shape your world.

From the title, you know we are talking about self-esteem. The cat is out of the bag now, so we might as well get right to it, shall we? Every man desires freedom; it explains why most wars fought in times past were about gaining liberty.

However, freedom is only attained first within and then in the external sense. Self-esteem is about being free enough to embrace all of you and still being in love with your own character. The idea of self-worth is essential to every man's growth in life. Hence the reason you must take all you learn in this book seriously.

The objective of this book is on the cover page; you will read tips on how to boost your confidence level, fight off low self-esteem, and live a depression-free life.

This material is divided into several chapters that are interwoven. The sections are structured in such a way that if you succeed with one tip, you will most likely do the same with the others. The objectives we have shared are achievable if you stick to everything you learn here.

Think about this book like a journey you have embarked on with a friend who is quite knowledgeable. Therefore, as a friend, I will advise you to grab a glass of your favourite drink, sit on the most comfortable couch you've got, and enjoy the ride. By the end of this book, you will learn how to become more knowledgeable, bold, fearless, and daring.

Your journey to becoming an Alpha Male begins with the first chapter on the principles of self-esteem. Take pleasure in reading, learning, and growing.

Chapter One

The Principles of Self-Esteem

I had never met Matthew in person until one rainy Wednesday afternoon when he walked into my office looking dejected. Matthew had called earlier to schedule a meeting - and from the expression on his face, I could tell he had a lot on his mind.

Matthew worked as a data analyst for a tech firm and felt like he had not done enough nor achieved anything tangible in all his years of work. Matthew found it very difficult to express himself at all times, and at some point, other people had begun to think it was a mental issue.

After spending time together, we discovered that Matthew's inability to follow through with anything was actually due to low self-esteem. Matthew had lived his whole life thinking there was someone else out there who was better than him.

Self-esteem is a critical aspect of life because it affects everything a person does or believes. Self-confidence is the feeling of satisfaction a man has about himself, knowing that he is not perfect but is good enough for the world. This is the feeling of respect, trust, and faith in one's abilities and judgement.

There is high and low self-esteem.

When a person has very high self-esteem, it means he has come to a place of complete acceptance of who he is and has managed to build a feeling of self-worth that cannot be tarnished.

On the other hand, a person with very low self-esteem struggles with feelings of self-worth, acceptance of self, and to believe in his ability to build great relationships with others. So, you either have a high self-esteem or a low one. If it is the former, you are in a good place; but if it is the latter, this book was written to guide you into making your life better.

Before we get to the sections that provide solutions, you must first understand why one can have either high or low self-esteem. No one is born with low self-esteem. Just like anything else, it is acquired through habit, relationships with others, and the situations a person is exposed to regularly.

Just the same, no one is born with high self-esteem. All men are made the same way, but the feelings they develop about themselves later in life stem from their experiences as children, teenagers, and adults.

In a bid to create excellent material on self-esteem, I had the privilege of interacting with people like Matthew, because I wanted to discover the root of the problem

Even if a person doesn't know that he has low self-esteem, from the moment the discovery is made, changes can begin. We have succeeded in considering two fundamental aspects thus far; firstly, that no one is born with high self-esteem, and secondly, that you can change how you feel about yourself.

You know some of the basic ideas. The next step is for you to become familiar with some of the principles of self-esteem.

The principles of self-esteem refer to some of the ideas that guide a person to become comfortable with himself. This is the first step to building self-esteem; you must be satisfied with who you are.

So what are the principles of self-esteem?

1.   Visualization

The first principle of self-worth and building self-esteem is to visualize what you want your life to be. When you discover what you are unhappy about and how you feel about yourself, instead of fussing about it, take time off every day to visualize yourself the way you want to be.

What do you see as your characteristics? What kind of person do you want to become? In your mind, replace the negatives with positives and start to live out the authentic self-esteem experience you see in your mind.

2.   Quiet Acceptance

This principle refers to the way you accept yourself for who you are. Oftentimes, we observe others and try to be like them. When we are consumed with the idea of being like someone else (often someone that we don't even know), we start to lose ourselves.

Quiet acceptance means you are aware of your flaws, you are in touch with your feelings, and you still accept yourself, regardless. This sense of satisfaction with oneself births ideas on how to become better; embrace all of you today!

3.   Patience with Self

I have seen cases of people who started on this journey to better self-esteem and didn't see it through to the end because they weren't patient enough. It took you time to get here so it will also take you time to detox.

So, make up your mind not to give up on yourself today. Stick to all of the steps and tips, work on yourself continuously, and build a tough skin that can withstand the challenges you face. For you to have enough self-esteem to be patient with others, you must first be patient with yourself.

4. Self-Protection

As you become more patient with yourself, also remember to protect yourself from negativity. The most peculiar cases of low self-esteem often stem from an inability to control negative vibes.

You should protect yourself from thoughts, ideas, and feelings that are not consistent with what you want or desire for yourself. You need to kick out whatever is not compatible with a positive mindset and then replace it with something good.

Self-protection should be taken seriously because whatever thoughts you feed your mind over time will manifest in your life and cause healing or damage.

5. Happiness over Anxiety

This is a choice you must make daily; am I going to be happy or anxious? You make this choice daily through the little decisions you make. It is proven that some of the most fortunate people on the planet have very high self-esteem.

Anxiety, on the other hand, makes you feel uncomfortable; it causes you to become irritable and angry over things you cannot control. Being anxious will never work for someone who wants to experience changes within himself.

Make up your mind today to be happy!

6.   The Power of Words

An essential principle for you to stick to is the power of words. On this quest toward better self-esteem, you will have to use affirmations to get the results you desire.

Say those lovely things you want to see manifest in your life and watch them become truth. If you used to say the wrong things before now, even jokingly, it is time to take a step back and re-evaluate your words.

Always let your speech be seasoned with grace; this will attract the right people to you and cause you to be kind to yourself, as well. When words are used correctly, they become transformative tools.

7.   Stick to Your Value System

Value systems are ideas we develop over time that help us maintain a certain standard of life. If you have value systems that have helped you shape your life in the most inspiring way possible, then now is the time to stick to them.

You shouldn't be moved by what everyone else is doing or what others adopt. Be determined to create your own rules and live by them. This is very important! People who are tossed around following other people's rules will never attain positive self-esteem.

Create a value system, stick to it and make it work; therein lies the pathway to high self-esteem.

Self-esteem is one of the most crucial yet underrated aspects of life. Everything a person will or will not achieve can be traced to how that person feels about himself. People with a very high perception of themselves tend to win all the time, not because they are somehow better, but because they believe in their abilities.

There is no telling how far one can go with very high self-esteem. It is akin to being the captain of a ship that is on course. Even if challenges come up later, the faith and hope you have built in yourself over time will help you put things in proper perspective and take the right steps.

Some of the principles discussed in this chapter will be presented in a very detailed form later, and we are starting with quiet acceptance. The next section contains lessons, tips, and valuable steps you can take toward cultivating high self-esteem via quiet acceptance. Do enjoy the read.

Chapter Two

Self-Acceptance; a Pathway to Cultivating High Self-Esteem

In discussing self-esteem, we must become aware of the role that self-acceptance plays. The previous section introduced you to some of the most basic concepts about the principles of self-worth - and quiet acceptance was listed.

Most cases of low self-esteem that manifest in people are as a result of a rejection of self, due to a feeling of being incomplete. If I build a house, I won't invite my friends over to the edifice until I feel it is 100% complete The same thing applies to us.

We often do not feel like we are enough. As such, we try to hide our most exact feelings because, just like the incomplete house, we feel as though we are not worthy of admiration or capable of doing anything right. We resort to self-rejection, and this affects our self-esteem.

Now that you have decided to build your self-esteem, you must be willing also to accept all of you. Now, I'm not talking about only the best sides; I'm talking about all of you! No individual is born perfect, with every good trait. Some traits are acquired, others are impacted into you, and some others are inherited.

However, regardless of the traits you embody, you must appreciate who you are before you can start the process of developing your self-esteem. You are a unique personality; there is no one like you in your world. As such, you owe it to yourself to have very high self-esteem;

one that allows you embrace every aspect of your life and live beyond your flaws.

Self-acceptance and self-esteem are not the same, but one leads to the other. If you love yourself well enough, there is an increasing chance that you will be able to build high self-esteem.

Self-acceptance is unconditional.

If you want to improve your self-esteem, you will need to explore the parts of yourself you are unable to accept. So, first you must stop passing judgement on yourself. Stop being so hard on yourself when you don't meet the expectations and targets you've set.

Self-acceptance can be traced back to the experiences a person has as a child. As a young child, you probably didn't know anything about self-worth or self-esteem, so this is where your parents or guardians played a crucial role.

If your parents did a good job of making you feel unique, independent, and complete, you wouldn't have any challenge with self-love as an adult. The foundation was already laid.

However, if you were brought up in an environment where it seemed like nothing you did was right - an environment of constant abuse and lack of motivation, you would most likely develop a critical mindset about yourself.

The most refreshing idea thus far is the fact that you can cultivate self-acceptance. It is possible to learn how to embrace who you are and live in the moment while building up your self-esteem.

So, can we get right to the steps you'll take toward making this right? We will start now.

How to Become More Self-Accepting

1. Cultivate Self-Compassion

A person who wants to be self-accepting must be compassionate toward himself. Often, we show compassion to others, but we don't show the same to ourselves.

So, we make a mistake and boom! We criticise and even abuse ourselves emotionally. Be compassionate and kind to yourself by tolerating your flaws and excesses.

2. Be Inspired by Your Past and Not by Other People

You can build positive self-esteem when you are inspired by your own history. The only person you are in competition with is yourself. Your only goal is to outdo your past self. Ensure that at every turn, you are focused on yourself and not on others.

In order to be self-accepting, you must celebrate your past achievements and then look forward to achieving more in the future. If you are fixated on others, you will be putting yourself under intense pressure to become like them. This is not a good move toward cultivating self-esteem.

3. Forgive Yourself

People who struggle with self-acceptance often have issues forgiving themselves for the wrongs of the past. If you don't forgive yourself, you will always be held down by these thoughts.

Be willing to forgive what you've done to yourself as well as to others. Forgiveness is a powerful tool that can help you become more self-accepting. Do not deflate your self-esteem by holding a grudge against yourself.

4. Make Changes (When Necessary)

There may be some areas of your life you want to change, especially concerning how you work or react to circumstances, or in your relationships with others. Be bold enough to make changes when such changes are needed.

If you leave things the way they are (especially when they are not right), you will be fuelling the dissatisfaction you have with your life and getting upset over something you have the power to change.

5. Be Happy with Yourself

Happiness is free; please take advantage of it! You must be extremely happy and satisfied with yourself to experience self-acceptance. Happiness is empowering, especially in your journey toward building self-esteem.

Share your happiness with others, as well. Create a world full of cheer -and don't stop until your whole world lights up with joy and the quiet acceptance of yourself.

If you aren't mindful of how well you accept yourself, you just might become so critical of your actions that it leads to self-resentment. This book is a practical one - and that explains why there are many steps for each tip.

The best gift you can give yourself is bringing these words to life through constant practice. As you read, make up your mind to act on what you discover. You will become what you repeatedly do; so make a commitment to your journey toward better self-esteem today by becoming more accepting of yourself.

Living purposefully is the next stop on our journey; discover the connection between purposeful living and self-esteem in the next chapter.

Chapter Three

How to Live Purposefully

Living purposefully refers to the idea that a person is living for a goal or purpose that acts as a driving force every day. A life of purpose is a life lived from the inside out where dreams and aspirations become a reality.

Whenever I speak about purposeful living, I liken it to a person embarking on a road trip. A driver needs to have a destination in mind while navigating through the routes with a reliable map.

Now, if the driver does not have an idea where he is headed, the trip will be a futile attempt and accomplish nothing. A purposeful life is one with a sense of direction; you have a goal in front of you, and wake up every day taking strategic steps towards accomplishing that goal.

So at this point, I know you are wondering what this has to do with building self-esteem. Well, the answer to your inquiry is the aim of this chapter. You will discover the connection between self-esteem and living purposefully while adopting approaches that help you discover your purpose, thus giving your self-esteem a significant enhancement.

As opposed to popular opinion, the purpose of life isn't just to be happy. Of course, happiness is essential, but the most important thing about living is making a difference in your own life and that of others by fulfilling your purpose. This also means that you must discover your purpose before filling it.

When you discover what you should be doing with your life, you will have a broader sense of appreciation for yourself, thus enhancing your self-esteem. A person who is oblivious of his purpose in life will live a very defeated life; he will be at the mercy of chance, and this deflates self-esteem.

Think about it this way; someone who has discovered their reason for living wakes up filled with optimism knowing that he can do so much more with his life. So, he goes about his day conscious of his abilities and making changes while being excited about life.

On the other hand, a person without a sense of purpose wakes up feeling uninspired and unsure about his abilities. He doesn't know if he can do all that is required of him. This makes him feel less confident - and we all know that confidence is a significant ingredient in building high self-esteem.

The importance of living purposefully cannot be overemphasised.

You will discover steps you can take toward living purposefully such that your self-esteem is on a stable level. But first, you must provide answers to questions that will help you discover your purpose, as well as what it means for a person to live with a sense of direction. After this process, we will discuss tips on how to live purposefully and build high self-esteem.

Are you ready to take on this step our journey? I hear your loud yes!! Let's get started with some questions.

For you to live a purposeful life, you must ask yourself specific questions. The answers to these questions will serve as the compass you require to determine your purpose. Find these queries below:

1. What do I want to achieve?
2. How do I achieve it?

3. Are there steps I must take toward achieving it?
4. Does my environment have a role to play?
5. Is there novel information I need to adopt?
6. Should I adjust my strategies?
7. Who will help me fulfil this goal?
8. How long will it take?
9. What do I have to give up achieving it?
10. How can I sustain this purpose?

For a more meaningful experience working with these questions, you will need to get a journal where you can document your answers. After reading through this chapter, go back to the issues and answer honestly. Your answers will point you in the direction of how you should live your life.

What Does it Mean to Live with Purpose?

Lots of indicators show what living purposefully entails. Below, we will take on a few. Remember that all of these approaches are building up to helping you improve your self-esteem. So, for a person to live purposefully, he must take note of the following:

1. Oversee formulating goals consciously.
2. Identify and implement actions that are necessary for the achievement of set goals.
3. Monitor behavioural traits to determine if they align with your goals.
4. Pay close attention to the results of your actions; it will help you determine whether you are making progress or not.

With purpose, you must continuously ask yourself: how do I move from here to get there? You also need to determine sub-purposes that will help you accomplish your goal.

Now to the big one! How can all these lessons you've learned become instrumental in helping you overcome low self-esteem and become the fearless Alpha-male you want to be? Read on; it gets better from this point.

How to Boost Self-Esteem by Living a Purposeful Life

1. Go for Your Goals Ferociously
You can defeat low self-esteem through purposeful living and going after your purposes fiercely. People with low self-esteem are mostly afraid of attacking their goals, and as such, they never accomplish anything.

You can improve your self-esteem by making sure your goals are a top priority through purposeful living. As you take deliberate steps toward achieving your purpose in life, you will be building an unshakeable self-esteem.

Let your goals inspire you to greatness as you live out your dreams every day.

2. Learn from Failures and Move On
As you become attuned with your goals, rest assured that you will make mistakes (this is how life works). Now, this is the problem with errors; some people become so upset by their failures that they don't want to try anymore.

When you allow failures to get the better part of your mind, you will experience low self-esteem. First, you need to tell yourself that it is okay to make mistakes, and even to fail - then make up your mind to move on from these mistakes.

Once you develop a positive mind-set toward failure, it will never have a hold over how you feel about yourself. Be open about failures; make them a part of your experience and learn.

3. Be Focused on the Future

Purposeful living entails being focused on the future. It is all about what you can do today to guarantee tomorrow's success. So, you must become consumed with the idea of having a better future.

Your self-esteem will get to a stable level when you become conscious of the fact that you can effect changes in your future now. It's like having superpowers - and superheroes have great self-esteem, right?

Always keep the future in focus; it will help you become an optimistic person who isn't afraid. The absence of fear means the presence of very good self-esteem.

4. Optimism is a Tool

Speaking of optimism, did you know that it is a tool? Oh yes, it is! Confidence is a tool that can be used to boost self-esteem while pursuing a life of purpose.

Individuals with low self-esteem will always be pessimistic, because they lack confidence. The solution is simple; get rid of the defeatist attitude, replace it with a cheerful disposition, and watch your self-esteem rise like an edifice.

Positivity will take you further; it will always make it possible for you to look beyond present obstacles and have a solution-driven mindset.

5. Always Aim High

If you are keen on living a purposeful life, that translates into great self-esteem. You must be willing to aim higher. Don't settle for less when you can have so much more.

The higher you aim, the more confident you become, thus boosting your self-esteem. Aiming high also means that mediocrity isn't allowed; you can only do things excellently and continue to build on the standard you create.

Life gets better with high goals, but you must be consistent with these goals. As you take on new assignments, your desire to be the best will help you make improvements in your self-esteem.

6.   Be in Control of Your Decisions

Being in control of your choices is a significant indicator that you have developed great self-confidence. Remember that this is your life and you must be willing to take charge.

A lack of controlled decision-making skills can lead to an absence of belief in one's ability to win in life. And this is a significant deal-breaker when considering self-esteem.

Trust in your ability to make the right decisions at all times, and remember what we talked about when we mentioned embracing mistakes. Even when you fail, never lose sight of the impact your choices have on your self-esteem.

7.   Celebrate Your Wins

Above all, always celebrate your successes. Regardless of how little they may be, be happy with your milestones and be conscious of how far you have come, while always hoping for the best.

If you make a habit of celebrating your wins, you will observe a significant boost in your self-esteem. Celebrating your successes means you appreciate all the effort you've put in; this is a major self-esteem booster.

Be the person who embraces all his journeys; the highs and lows are a significant part of your experience, so be grateful for the former while staying optimistic for more of the latter.

We have succeeded in establishing a connection between self-esteem and living with purpose. There is so much for you to achieve when you know exactly what you are meant to do with your life. As you set yourself on fire with your goals, you will also be giving your self-esteem the boost it requires.

All the strategies you have gleaned in this chapter will only become effective when you start implementing them immediately. As you do, be mindful of the lessons you learn and use your experience to help someone else grow. We will be considering happiness in a moment; flip over to the next chapter to get all the scoop.

Chapter Four

Getting Rid of Happiness Anxieties

Happiness is crucial to living a great life. This is the reason a lot of self-help books always insist on the principle of being happy. If everyone could be happy forever, the world will be a better place. Some issues may come up that affect the quality of a person's happiness.

When a person isn't pleased, they will have to deal with low self-esteem. So in this chapter, we will deal with a significant concept that affects a person's happiness. We are talking about happiness anxieties.

Happiness anxieties can also be referred to as the fear of being happy, and it is a significant cause of low self-esteem. When a person is happy and fulfilled with life, they will always be optimistic, thus building up a great feeling of self-acceptance.

However, some people who have had hurtful experiences in the past try to justify why they shouldn't be happy. As such, they gradually build resistance toward being happy. This gives room for anxiety, panic attacks, and fear, all of which are factors that affect a person's self-esteem.

Happiness anxieties take time to build. It may start as a thought and then gradually increase to a feeling of discontent that triggers overall sadness. All of these negative emotions culminate into a person becoming sceptical of happiness.

The most vital point you should note here is this; happiness anxieties will affect your self-esteem in the most negative ways. What we should consider now is how to get rid of this feeling for good.

This chapter is a straightforward and practical one; you will discover steps you can take toward getting rid of your happiness anxiety. Please note that if you have been dealing with this anxiety for a while, it may take you a long time to get out of it. But if you are committed to the tips, they will work for you. Let's get started!

Note that for every step you will encounter below, there is an exercise you must carry out. Think of the activity as an accountability test that helps ensure you do what is required of you through the steps.

How to Get Rid of Happiness Anxieties

1. Think Happy Thoughts
First, you need to ensure that you are always thinking happy thoughts. Come on, how else will you fight off happiness anxieties if not with happy thoughts? You have got to be deliberate about this!

You cannot afford the luxury of one bad thought, so take it seriously. With happy thoughts, you can be sure of taking satisfactory actions that boost how you feel about yourself.

So, every day, there is a battle in your mind of the thoughts that will prevail; happy or sad feelings.

Exercise:
Every day, censor your thought process by ensuring that it is in line with what makes you happy. Whenever you feel like you are dwelling on an uninspiring thought, get it out of your mind and replace the

idea with a happy one. Do this consistently, and you will be able to gain mastery over your thoughts.

2. Share Your Joy with Others

Life is worth living when you can share simple pleasures with others. As you think happy thoughts, share the feelings of joy with others around you. Those with very high self-esteem always have a touch, smile, or word of kindness for someone else.

You will be able to build very high self-esteem by being involved in the lives of others. And more importantly, this is one way of kicking out happiness anxiety.

Exercise:
What can you share with someone close to you? Think about how you can put a smile on that person's face - and go right ahead and do it. Remember that building self-esteem isn't just about what you do, but what you do for others.

3. Take the Pressure off Yourself

As you share your joy, remember to take the weight of pleasing others off yourself. In a bid to make everyone else happy, we put a great deal of pressure on ourselves. This affects our level of self-esteem.

At all times, remember to be yourself. It is okay to try your best for others - but not at the expense of mounting pressure on yourself unnecessarily.

Happiness anxieties will start to kick in when you put yourself under undue pressure. The exercise below will help you avoid this pitfall.

Exercise:
Whenever you start to feel pressured, take a deep breath, sit in a tranquil place, close your eyes, and take your mind off the pressure. After a few minutes, analyse the reason you feel pressured and deal with it by either getting rid of it or doing happily what can be done.

4. Choose to Say No

We just analysed the reason you shouldn't put yourself under pressure, but did you know that the urge to say yes to everyone is a form of coercion?

You are not obligated to listen to and endorse what everyone says, or else you will lose yourself in a bid to please them. One of the traits evident in people with low self-esteem is their inability to speak out, especially when they aren't comfortable with something.

Exercise:
The next time someone asks you for something or requests that you do something for them, search your inner self to decide if it is something you really want to do. Now, if you are excited about doing it, go right ahead. On the contrary, if you aren't so enthusiastic about it, make that clear to the person making the request. Saying NO is up to you!

5. See the Good in Yourself

There are good things you embody. Oh, I hope you will see all of you through your own eyes. When people see only their wrongs, they shrink in confidence.

We will speak more on embracing your flaws in the next step, but before we get there, I want you to become aware that you are blessed with a lot of great attributes. These great qualities you have will make you feel good about yourself.

Exercise:
Take some time to reflect on your life, identify those good things about yourself, and ensure that you amplify them by acting on them often.

6. Embrace Your Imperfections

Everyone is created with flaws, and if you are unable to embrace your faults, you will always seek perfection and be dissatisfied with your inability to attain it.

Be so in love with yourself that there is no room for self-condemnation. It is okay to look up to people you admire, but don't beat yourself up trying to be perfect.

Exercise:
What are those areas you feel are your imperfections? Enjoy them today; they are a part of your life, so embrace them. The people you think have great self-esteem also have shortcomings, but they have been able to accept such flaws. Hence the reason they are so confident.

7. Be Conscious of Your Moods

Most times, feelings of anxiety manifest through our spirits. If you are always prone to severe mood swings, you will most likely experience happiness anxieties.

By paying attention to your moods, you can tell when you are sad, happy, or angry. Once you can tell how you are feeling, you will know how to adjust your mood to suit your goal of being happy.

Exercise:
How are you feeling now? Happy? Disappointed? Sad? Fulfilled? If you are in a happy mood, then keep up with the activities and thoughts that make you feel happy. If you are experiencing negative

feelings, discover why you have such feelings and deal with them now.

8. Engage in Happy Activities
How important this is!

Happiness anxieties cannot thrive in an environment with peaceful activities. However, happy actions do not just happen. You've got to actively participate in them every day.

Happy activities vary from person to person. For some people, exercise makes them feel uplifted, while for some others, hanging out with friends work just fine. For you, it might be reading a book. But whatever it is, ensure that you do it often.

Exercise;
Think of an activity that makes you happy - and get on with it right now. Set a schedule to do it regularly within a specified period and you will be glad you did.

9. Be Kind to Yourself
We are raised to be helpful to others, to treat them well, and to be models of goodness to all those around us. But the real question is, are we kind to ourselves? Do we love who we are and who we have become?

It is so important to exercise kindness toward yourself, or else you will look for it in others. And when they fail to give it to you, you tend to suffer low self-esteem. Those things you do for others that exhibit kindness - do them to yourself as well.

Check on your emotions, buy gifts for yourself, and be patient with who you are becoming.

Exercise:
Use the remainder of the day to perform acts of kindness to yourself. Do something you have never done for yourself and watch your self-esteem get a significant boost.

10. Make Happy Decisions

The kind of decisions you make determine if you will be able to get rid of happiness anxiety. You must always be deliberate about making choices that cause you to be happy.

Of course, there will be times you will be required to make some decisions you are not entirely happy about. But, if MOST of your personal choices are happy ones, it will go a long way toward helping you retain happiness, thus building healthy self-esteem.

Exercise:
What decisions are you making at this very moment? Think of one and go back and review your desire to make this decision. Be sure that it is one you will be happy with long term. After reviewing your willingness to make the choice, only go through with what makes you happy. Get on this task now!

11. Be Comfortable with Your Life

Being satisfied with your life doesn't mean you shouldn't aspire to be and do more. It just means that you appreciate where you are right now and look forward to getting more out of life.

However, the key concept here is being happy with where you are in life. A lot of times, people develop poor self-esteem because they wish to become more like someone else. They are not satisfied with their lives, so they seek validation from others.

The problem with seeking validation is this; you will end up being uncomfortable with your own life and then attempt live out other people's dreams, thus leading to a miserable experience.

For you to guard how you feel about yourself, you must be comfortable with whatever level you are at right now. Your ability to be comfortable shows strength of character and that is what having high self-esteem is all about.

Exercise:
Get your journal and make a list of all the things you are very comfortable and happy with in your life. Ensure that you look back as far as five years. After writing, give yourself a thumbs-up and smile at your accomplishments, knowing that it will get better going forward.

Happiness anxiety is one of the major causes of low self-esteem. It starts with a thought and then gradually becomes a part of the person's mental process. Ultimately, the individual begins to feel downcast, and this erodes them of high self-esteem.

With the tips you have been given above, you can fight off the feeling and deal with the issue of being anxious over being happy. We are now done with the chapter on happiness, and our next stop is putting you in focus. Self-awareness is crucial, but how important is it? Get some answers to this and more in the next chapter.

Chapter Five
Being Conscious of Self

Justin has always known that he isn't a party person. He loves to be indoors and enjoys spending time by himself. However, he's got friends who are the "life of a party"; these friends must hang out every Friday -and every other day.

So Justin makes it to events with his friends every weekend. And when he gets home, he feels like he has wasted time doing nothing because he isn't a party person. The case with Justin is simple; he isn't conscious of who he is at all.

If Justin continues to violate who he is to please his friends, he will lose track of himself. This can lead to a very severe case of low self-esteem. By continually leaning on others and believing in what they uphold without having his own opinion or taking a stance, Justin will end up with very low self-esteem and a lack of self-confidence.

Self-esteem is about having a view of yourself that allows you to feel great about who you are. It is a feeling that brings about confidence and a feeling of wholeness. But if a person isn't conscious of self, or isn't aware of who they are, there will be a problem.

Being self-conscious also means you have a sharp realization of your personality, strengths, weaknesses, beliefs, thoughts, motives, and emotions. When you are self-aware, you will be able to understand other people and discover how they perceive you, as well.

For you to be a man with very high self-esteem, you must first become aware of who you are. Now, this chapter is significant, so I will need you to pay very close attention.

When we speak of being self-aware, we refer to ideas around how well you know yourself. Make no mistakes about this; no one can attain high self-esteem without first knowing who they are. So here goes; WHO ARE YOU?

Take a few minutes to provide answers to that question.

Do you know who you are now? Do you know what you love? What do you appreciate about life? What can you not tolerate? What about the kind of people you relate easily with? How well do you know your emotions? How about your preferences? There are a whole lot of things you must consider when thinking about who you are.

If you do not get to know who you are, you will be a confused person who isn't able to hold his own anywhere. The key to building and maintaining high self-esteem is to discover who you are first - then ensure that the steps, actions, and activities you indulge in help bring out the best in who you are, thus aiding increased confidence.

In this chapter, you will come across two significant aspects. They include the benefits of being self-conscious and how a person can become self-aware. Beginning with the benefits, below you will find some of the reasons why it is essential for you to become self-aware.

The Benefits of Being Self-Conscious

1. It Helps You Become a Better Leader
Great leaders are self-conscious. They know that they must lead others, so they need to have a very firm grasp on their own strengths and weaknesses. As they discover themselves, they get to know more about those they lead.

2. Increases Self-Esteem

We are talking about how to build better self-esteem, so we are on course as we discover more about ourselves. When you are aware of who you are, your self-esteem will increase.

At this point, you are not trying to be like someone else; nor are you modelling your life after someone else's dream. So, if you are ready to feel better about yourself, then you must learn to discover who you are by being self-aware.

Get to know you; the real you!

3. You Tend to Build Better Relationships

With knowledge of who you are, you will also develop better relationships because you will spend time with people of like minds. Justin would have made better choices with his friends if he had stayed true to who he was.

It is so important that you spend time with people who are like you or have the same belief systems as you. Life becomes more comfortable when you know what you want and the people around you are on the same page as you.

The quality of your relationships will be determined by the kind of people you spend time with. Don't accept or encourage any relationship that makes you feel pressured enough to do things you don't want to do. Relationships should change you for the better.

4. You Make Better Decisions

When you are self-aware, you make better decisions. Some people make poor decisions based on who others are rather than on who they are. This affects the results they get in life.

Instead of being led to make wrong decisions by other people, invest in getting to know yourself. You will be grateful for the time you spent learning about yourself as it will lead to better, healthier, and wiser choices.

5. You Minimize Mistakes
Although mistakes are inevitable, if you get to know who you are, this makes it possible for you to reduce errors. Some mistakes can be avoided if you pay attention to who you are long enough.

The pathway to living a life with fewer mistakes is being in touch with the real you, and not forgetting that this also serves as a significant boost for your self-esteem.

Now that you know the importance of being self-aware, we can get right to the focus of this chapter; how to become self-aware.

Aside from asking yourself questions that will help you discover who you are, you can engage in some fascinating steps that will give insight into how you can become more self-aware. Now remember that it isn't enough for you to become aware of who you are, you must also live out your truth.

Justin knew who he was but didn't act on that knowledge. Instead, he was carried away by the desires and wants of the people around him. So below, you will read through some of the most effective steps you can take toward becoming self-aware.

How to Become Self-Aware to Build Healthy Self-Esteem

1. Practise Self-Reflection Every Day
When you practise self-reflection every day, you will be able to better stay connected with who you are. You can practise self-reflection by taking time out of your schedule to discover who you are and what you want in life.

A good way of reflecting and engaging in exercise is through yoga. If you are not a fan of yoga, then you might want to find a quiet corner in your home where you can think, reflect, and discover.

Sometimes, people read about self-reflection, do it for a week or two, and then put a stop to it; but it won't work like this. You've got to do it consistently to get the desired results.

More so, reflections can be done at the end of each day. Think about what happened to you and how the events of the day give an accurate picture of who you are.

2. Keep a Journal

Another way of being self-aware is keeping a journal. Now, this isn't a journal for secrets. I am talking about a memoir that chronicles your activities such that you can determine who you are from the entries.

If you are going to keep a journal, then it must be updated often. Write down important events and activities that happen and how you respond to them. These little efforts, if done repeatedly, will help you discover your true nature.

3. Work with Friends

Your friends see what you don't, sometimes. As such, it will be a great idea for them to provide feedback. Sometimes, we must look at ourselves through the eyes of someone else to know what we value and what we don't.

If you've got a great support system, you might want to have an assessment meeting with your friends. At such meetings, they will share their experiences and thoughts about you (the positives and negatives). You would do the same for them, so it's a balanced narrative.

At the end of such meetings, you will be amazed at all you will discover about yourself just by getting feedback from those nearest and dearest to you

4. Practise Meditation

We talked about reflecting earlier on, and that is entirely different from meditating. When you meditate, you keep your mind fixated on one thing, concept, or idea.

In this case, you will be meditating about your life. As you meditate, you will become aware of your inner powers and connect with yourself on a whole new level. That connection will help you maintain a great relationship with yourself that leads to very high self-esteem.

5. Be Objective with Yourself

Lastly, you've got to be objective with your self-assessment. Subjectivity will make you become biased towards yourself, and this won't help you on your journey to better self-esteem.

When you are objective, you will become real enough to point out your faults and be determined to work on them. Individuals who are objective tend to exhibit high self-esteem because they have conquered all fears.

If you are self-aware, you will be a man with very solid self-esteem. You will be able to embrace your strengths and weaknesses while staying true to who you are. In being conscious of who you are, you will require a very vital tool - the mind. Head over to the next section as you discover how the mind can be used in ensuring great self-esteem.

Chapter Six
Using the Mind as a Force Field

There is a connection between the mind and self-esteem.

You will ultimately become everything you think you are. So that means the mind is a forcefield that can be used to achieve desired results.

The mind is not a physical organ of the body, but a part of your make-up as a human being, and it contains information on all you think, dream and aspire to be. In your mind, you can become anything; whatever you feed it will show forth in your life.

This chapter takes us a step further in our journey by checking in with your psychological framework through the power of your mind. We will not make a lot of progress on this journey to better self-esteem if we don't consider the role the mind plays.

So, as you read through, get ready to discover some of the best ideas on how you can transform your life, kick depression out, and be the best version of all you can be, just by using your mind correctly.

A force field can serve as an invisible barrier that is used as a protective shield. Your mind can be a protective shield that keeps you safe from negative ideas that may affect your self-esteem.

There is so much to discuss in this chapter, and we will go through it because once you get it right in your mind, you get it right in every other aspect of your journey toward better self-esteem.

You should know that everything you experience in your life is as a result of what you have birthed in your mind. Have you ever thought about a person and then BOOM, you see that person within seconds of that thought? Well, that gives you an idea of how powerful the mind is. But more importantly, it teaches you the impact the mind has over everything you do.

Everyone is born with a mind, but not everybody can utilise it successfully. The mind can be trained and developed to function as a person wants it to; it is all about the kind of material you feed it.
So concerning self-worth, if you always tell yourself that you aren't good enough, you aren't worthy, and every other negative comment that doesn't add value to your experience, you will gradually begin to lose faith in yourself and develop a poor perception of who you are.

When we say the mind can be trained, what can we use as a tool to affect training?

Tools for Training the Mind

1. Words
Using words, you can feed your mind with negative or positive ideas that will determine the level of your self-esteem. You must have heard or been told about how you shouldn't use the wrong words on other people right?

Well, you really shouldn't use hurtful words on yourself, either. In a bid to be kind, ensure that you are always speaking kindly to yourself.

If your words do not teach or inspire you, they will settle in your mind like weeds in fertile soil. You may forget those cruel things you said, but the mind has absorbed them. Then, one day when you need motivation from within, instead of hearing the right words from your mind, those weeds speak up. And you already know that weeds are always up to no good.

Your self-esteem will develop in a positive light or diminish based entirely on your choice of words. You ought to listen attentively to yourself. What are you saying when no one else is around you? What do you mutter to yourself?

If you censor your words, you will also be able to protect your mind; and a guarded mind is a platform for increased self-esteem. Aside from the words you say to yourself, you should also be mindful of what others tell you. If you are always around people who bring you down with words, you may want to reconsider your circle.

A young man shared a story once of how he had to resign from his job because his boss was always verbally abusive toward him. So this boss knew that the young man was talented and good at his job but wouldn't want to give commendations.

At every turn, he found a way of bringing the young man down with hurtful and sarcastic comments. Gradually, this young man's self-esteem started to wane. The employee could no longer carry out tasks confidently; he had a lot of weeds in his mind as a result of all the negative words he heard.

When he resigned, he took time off to detoxify himself and replace those words that had destroyed his self-esteem with powerful affirmations that reminded him of who he was.

The mind is like a garden; your thoughts are the plants and words are like the water used to nurture the plant. However, if the words are not favourable, they become weeds that choke the garden and lead to deflated self-esteem.

Today, decide to only listen to the kind words because of the sanity of your mind. Say the right things to yourself, as well. Now, aside from words, there is another tool that is used for training the mind. You will find it below.

2. Images

The mind uses pictures to bring ideas to your consciousness. If you have been to Paris before and you want to tell someone about your experience, you will probably first think about the Eiffel Tower. That image will spur you on to narrate your experiences.

You see that the image of the tower remains stuck in your mind because it is indeed a sight to behold. The pictures in your mind also go a long way in determining how you feel about yourself.

There is a viral photo of a cat looking at a mirror, and the reflection it sees is that of a lion. This photo aptly captures the power of images to the mind. That cat will always move and act like a lion. It is fearless and utterly confident because the image it sees in the mirror inspires faith.

It isn't about what the reality is when we are dealing with the mind. Instead, it is all about what you see and perceive to be real. So, if you see yourself as a failure who isn't going to achieve much, then rest easy knowing that whatever is left of your self-esteem will be destroyed.

Ensure that at every chance you get, you show your mind uplifting images of yourself. You've got to be deliberate about this; don't allow the wrong picture to settle in the force field of your mind.

We have already established the fact that self-esteem is a crucial ingredient for success. As such, if you are going to succeed, you must be willing to protect your mind at all costs.

Now, images can also come from the media; sometimes the media likes to portray men as being weak especially in a world where lots of women are beginning to shatter glass ceilings. As you read through what the media offers, make sure you filter the images that settle in your mind.

When your mind is free from negative words and images, you will be able to truly live out your potential as an Alpha male who is fearless and willing to take on the world.

In dealing with the mind, we should also consider the role of mental health, because this plays a considerable role in shaping how you feel about yourself.

Words and images are tools you can use in shaping the narrative within your mind; once you've got great words and images, you must start thinking about how you can improve your self-esteem using the right frame of mind.

How to Use the Mind to Improve Your Self-Esteem

1. Learn to be Assertive
Being assertive means you don't have ideas and words you want to share clogged up in your mind. It means you can speak and say precisely what you want to say at any time.

As an assertive person, your mind will be free of insecurity, and you will become bold enough to speak and share your thoughts confidently. As you speak with boldness, your self-esteem receives a significant boost, and that is what you need to become fearless and daring.

2. Focus on the Positives
You can use your mind as a tool for focus. Be mindful of the positive things that happen around you and feed your mind with such details.

Whatever you focus on consistently will have a significant impact on how your mind embraces the idea of having improved self-esteem. Make it a routine to delete all traces of negative energy or thoughts at the end of each day.

Welcome every new day with optimism and a renewed desire to get the best out of your mind. Improving on your self-esteem is a process; work at it every single day and enjoy the results afterwards.

3. Recreate Your World

It is possible to recreate your world if you are not satisfied with what you experience currently. For some people, they've got a positive mindset, but their personal lives do not correspond with what they envision in their minds.

If you are not happy with what you've got now, have a reorientation of the mind and recreate your world. Your mind can become a world of possibility and reality to you; use it to fire up your self-esteem, and you will be grateful you did.

4. Fall in Love with Yourself

Love makes everything alright with the world, and love can give you the self-esteem boost you require. So, now you need to love yourself more than ever before. We will elaborate more on how you can fall in love with yourself in a later chapter, so look out for that.

As you love yourself, you will discover all those great things about you that you appreciate and that make you feel good about yourself. People who are in love with themselves do not bring themselves down with hurtful words.

Let your mind become a force field of love that is nurtured and groomed in such a way that there is no room for anything contrary. Love is the most powerful emotion that can transform a man's life. But more importantly, self-love is crucial to adopting high self-esteem.

5. Create Mental Boundaries

Mental boundaries refer to the barricades you set up that prevent the wrong ideas, images, and thoughts to breed in your mind.

Because your mind is all-powerful, you need to be sure that only the good stuff gets in.

Your mental boundaries can be counter-words and actions that repel the effect of the wrong things on your mind. For every unhappy thought that tries to get to your mind, counter it with a happy thought; this is how you use mental boundaries to protect your mind and boost self-esteem.

If the mind is nurtured and protected, it can be used as an instrument for improved self-esteem. With the information you have received in this chapter, the onus lies on you now to ensure that your mind is not left to roam freely, accepting any image or word.

Once you create mental boundaries, recreate the world you desire, and fall in love with yourself, you will be able to use your mind to improve your self-esteem. Remember to focus on the positives while learning how to be assertive. The next section reaffirms the power you hold as an individual; it is one section you don't want to miss.

Chapter Seven

You are Enough!

One of the reasons some people suffer from very low self-esteem is because they don't think they are enough and they always seek validation from others.

The issue of seeking validation from others was mentioned briefly in a previous chapter, but here we will analyse it thoroughly. People do not enjoy the benefits of self-esteem because they are looking at someone else and thinking that what that person has is what they need to feel complete.

So the struggle for wholeness begins, and the further the journey goes, the more such individuals imitate others, the more they lose themselves in the process. What is left of them is a man who is afraid, tired, and depressed - because no one can be like someone else.

We are all born with unique traits and abilities. What you can do if you are not satisfied with what you have is to improve on yourself, so you become better instead of trying to be like somebody else. Hear me say this to you now; YOU ARE ENOUGH!!

There is no one else like you in the world! That should be enough reason for your self-esteem to be at a very high level. The temptation to be like someone else will only drive you into losing your originality.

When you start to exhibit the traits of someone else, you will develop a deep feeling of dissatisfaction because you realise that you are only an imitation and not an original. The world has embraced technology, and through avenues such as social media, we are exposed to many people who live false lives.

Here you are being authentic and real with your story, and then because you follow this person on Instagram, who seems to have a "perfect life," you suddenly feel like you don't have anything.

The quest to imitate someone with the perfect life begins, and as you try to do your best with the information dished out on social media, you lose the essential part of your life that makes you unique. I am not saying that you shouldn't be on social media, but be mindful of what you adopt because it may affect your self-esteem in the long term.

Always tell yourself that you are enough. You may not be where you want to be, but you are not where you used to be. An important criterion needed for a person who wants to have very high self-esteem is to be content with who he is.

There is so much power in being happy with who you are; it not only helps you gain improved self-esteem, it also enables you to experience satisfaction with your life in general.

No matter how much I tell you that you are enough, it will not make a lot of impact unless you believe it and say it to yourself as well. A deeper appreciation of who you are will be instrumental in helping you build and sustain a great self-image.

Being enough also means that you like yourself (this is a more straightforward way to put it). You have got to be comfortable in your skin, smile at the mirror more, and generally love who you are - because it is only when you accept yourself that you can start building great self-esteem.

So, what can you do to internalise this message of being enough? Oh, you can do a whole lot; and we are getting to it right now. Below, you will read through the top eight strategies you can practise and adopt that which will help you like yourself more, so you can say you are enough and mean it.

Top Eight Steps on How to Like Yourself and Develop High Self-Esteem

1. Talk to Yourself as a Friend

One of the steps toward loving yourself and reinforcing the message of being enough is by talking to yourself as you would a good friend. As a friend to yourself, emphasise those traits and attributes you embody that make you unique.

When your friend continually gives you compliments, it boosts your confidence and aids in building better self-esteem, too. So, don't wait for your friend to tell you who you are. Be a friend to yourself; be your own best friend.

As you show kindness through words to yourself, you will always be content with who you are while improving on the areas you should work on.

2. Lower Expectations

When your expectations are too high, you will never feel like you are enough. Overly high expectations will make you feel like you are inadequate; and this negatively affects self-esteem.

Sometimes, it pays to lower your expectations - especially with ideas that will make you do things you aren't comfortable with, to meet up with the standards of other people.

Vet every expectation you have by ensuring that it is in line with what you want for your life and not some dream inspired by the need to be like someone else.

When expectations are lowered, you also get to appreciate the value of experience. Instead of rushing off to accomplish things, you will take pride in learning and growing through the process.

3. Visualise Yourself Getting Better

The key to liking yourself even more is in utilising the power of visualisation. You have to first see yourself the way you want to be before you can become that image.

Always visualise yourself getting better, increasing your capacity, and living an inspiring life. Most people do not use their minds to create the pictures they desire, so there is usually a gap between what they want and what they experience.

As you visualise, you also reposition yourself to take strategic steps to bring the visions to reality.

4. Discover Who You Are

The only way you will learn to like yourself is by discovering who you are. You cannot want or love what you don't know; and regardless of how old you are, it is possible that you haven't discovered yourself yet.

This step is so important! You need to spend time discovering everything about yourself, so when you say "I am enough" it is said with authority.

You can discover who you are by spending time with yourself, analysing your responses to situations, and getting to know the kind of things you like. Once you find out how awesome you are, you will fall in love with yourself.

5. No Regrets

Regrets have a way of diminishing your self-esteem, especially when you fester on them for too long. So, make up your mind not to have regrets over situations you cannot control.

There will be times when you make mistakes; what you should do is learn from them and move on. The more you dwell on regrets, the more your self-esteem is affected negatively.

Make up your mind today to live a life that is without regrets. Whatever you experience is not a failure; it is only a lesson that will inspire you to become a better person.

6. Gratitude is a Lifestyle

In life, there will be ups and downs. But one thing is for sure, if you make gratitude a lifestyle, you will be amazed at how far you'll come. Be grateful for the little things, because the little things put together make the big things work.

Express gratitude to those who make the process easier for you, and be grateful for the challenges as well. Recognition helps you build and sustain great self-esteem, because you become aware of your imperfections and still appreciate your journey.

7. Use Affirmations

Oh, I love this step - because it works all the time. With statements, you can bring all you dream about, imagine, or desire to life. I always advise people to have an affirmation book that contains words about what they want.

Every day, they say these words to themselves, and it forms the basis on which their self-esteem lies. Affirmations are not said so you'll believe them; they are said because you already have faith in your words.

If you have struggled with being punctual in the past, you can write affirmations that state how early you always are to events. Gradually, you will observe that you are indeed becoming a punctual person.

If you feel like you are dealing with low self-esteem, then now is the time to write out affirmations that express high self-esteem. Keep saying what you believe, and it will become a part of you eventually.

8. Bring Out the Good in You
As you discover and affirm who you are, take steps toward bringing out the very best in yourself. Men with very high self-esteem showcase the good within them in the most humbling ways.

If you are good at something and you find yourself in a place where such skills are needed, don't shy away from offering to help. Speak up and do your best to make a difference. As you do these little things for others, you will be building confidence in yourself

Once you tell yourself that you are enough, repeatedly, it will become a truth that you endorse and believe. Your self-esteem will also experience a significant boost as you bask in the thrill of being enough.

No one should have to aspire to be somebody else. Yes, you can admire people and want to emulate them; but don't desire to copy them entirely, because you are an original. As you maintain your stance on being enough, be prepared to fight and win the war within; this and more await you in the next section. Do enjoy the read.

Chapter Eight

Winning the War Within

If there is anything Ashton doesn't like about deciding, it is the process of choosing what to do at a given time. So, whenever he is faced with a tough choice to make, he tries to avoid it; and this is a sign of very low self-esteem.

The more Ashton avoids issues that require him making a choice, the more his self-esteem wanes. Ashton's inability to decide stems from the fact that he hasn't dealt with the war that rages on within him.

Until he wins that war, he will be plagued by indecisiveness, which happens to be a factor associated with low self-esteem. There are a lot of Ashton's in the world today. People who struggle with themselves daily are unable to get anything done.

The first concept you should grasp here is simple; there is a war that rages on inside you. If you don't manage it appropriately, you will make uninformed decisions and sometimes fail to make any decision at all. What is this war really about?

Well, within you, there is a feeling of being torn between what you should do and what is expected of you. This war is usually a result of what you knew while growing up, your present environment, and what you know right now.

When you are faced with a problem, your first impulse is to think about what to do. You may not want to say the first idea that popped in your head, because you are trying to be careful. But, the more you shy away from making a decision, the more vulnerable you become, and the less you accept yourself.

There is always a constant battle from within that makes us appear confused, thus making it easy for people to take advantage of us. People will want to ride on the fact that you are always indecisive. Your ability to win the war will determine if you can protect yourself from them, as well as become a man who knows what he wants and goes for it.

In this chapter, you will be armed with steps to win the battle from within. You will be faced with other external factors, but if you can take care of what's within, then every other aspect can be handled.

How to Win the Battle Within

1. Know What You Want
Confusion and an inability to make great choices stems from the fact that people do not know what they want. When you see what you want and embrace the totality of your choices, you will be taking the first step toward winning the internal battle.

So, as you reflect and discover who you are, also get to know the things you want. When faced with the task of deciding, you will know exactly what to say and what to choose.

An Alpha Male isn't held down by indecision; your responsibility is to fight it off entirely by knowing what you want and going for it.

2. Say It as It Is
When you discover what you want, the next step will be for you to say it as it is when asked. The funny faces we make when we are asked a simple question are an indication that we are stalling because we are unable to express ourselves.

The war within causes you to ignore what you want to say because you are concerned with what people will think. Well, you really cannot become a great person with high self-esteem if you are always worried about what people think. Say what you want to say and damn the consequences.

3. Be Known for Being Confrontational

A lot of times, we are held back from building self-esteem because we try to avoid being confrontational. Instead, we murmur and talk behind others' backs - which is a bad trait.

People with very high self-esteem are known to look others in the eye and say what they want to say. When you are confrontational, you will always live freely with others.

Being confrontational makes it easy for you to be straightforward with others, thus building your self-esteem. Don't hold the grudge you've got for someone else. Walk up to them and solve issues; it is the hallmark of high self-esteem.

4. Don't Hold Yourself Back

At times when you need to express yourself, nothing should hold you back. Think about yourself at this point like a bird that is free to fly. Nothing should clip your wings, so hop on the side of self-esteem.

The more you let yourself go, the more likely you are to improve your self-confidence. The key to being happy with yourself is to live freely; once you conquer this, every other thing falls into place.

As we round off this sub-section, remember to be free; it is a significant requirement for success on this self-esteem journey.

5. Make Smaller Decisions

Sometimes you dive right into making big decisions without first conquering the smaller ones. When you gain mastery over smaller decisions, you will be able to make the bigger ones with ease.

What to wear, what to eat, or what to do with your spare time are examples of small decisions. These are choices you make every day; so use them as opportunities to develop a stronger mindset towards decision-making.

6. Stick to What You Say
Often, we say something, and then we go back on it because we are not confident enough in ourselves. So, there are cases of people who say what they want to say, then when they are confronted before a larger audience, they deny their statement.

The solution to this challenge is quite simple; stick to what you say. If you want to avoid the devastating effect of being unsure about what you mean to people, own up to your statements.

Be known as a person who is always bold enough to make decisions and speak up regardless of what you are faced with. Your ability to stick to what you say is an indication of your high self-esteem.

7. Drown the Voice of Doubt
The voice of doubt will always be heard, but you should not give in to it. Whatever you decide, you will always feel unsure at some point. But you must drown that voice and not allow it to reign over your mind.

Self-esteem is about self-control and acceptance of one's own views. You cannot say you accept your views when your mind is filled with doubt. Get doubts off your mind by ensuring that you maintain a stern approach to everything you believe in.

Doubt makes you question everything and while having such questions is normal, nursing questions that make you lack faith in yourself is not ideal.

8. Be Firm with Others
People with low self-esteem tend to allow others to ride on them. You must be firm in the relationships you build with others. It is okay to accept suggestions from people, but when you make a final decision, be FIRM!

Do not be easily persuaded and tossed about doing the biddings of other people;, only people with low self-esteem live like that. When you show firmness with every decision you make, you will be able to build up great self-esteem.

9. Exude Confidence in Decision Making
While sharing your ideas with others via decision making, exude confidence. Always speak with clarity and look into others' eyes while you speak. You will be taken more or less seriously based on how confidently you express yourself.

The battle within is always based on what you should say, do, or accept -and confidence is one tool that will help you win. Faith isn't just about how you speak, but also about your body language.

If you speak with your shoulders slumped and eyes looking down, you will appear as someone who can be manipulated easily.

I know this book is replete with information on the role that confidence plays in building self-esteem, but this is because confidence and self-esteem are two peas in a pod; one cannot do without the other.

10. Trust Your Instincts
Your instincts will always be right. The thing about winning the battle within is the fact that you are not entirely helpless. You've got several tools at your disposal, and your instincts are one of such devices.

Whenever you are in doubt, rely on what your instincts tell you and use them to make your final decision. If you have trained your mind well to accept right over wrong, your abilities will never lead you in the wrong direction.

You have all you need to believe in yourself and trust the process.

The battle within is all about how you make decisions because your decision-making skills reflect how high or low your self-esteem is. People who are known for making great choices often show very high self-esteem, and you can too if you stick to the steps provided above.

Remember that the journey to improved self-esteem is a gradual one that entails a lot of work. You have read and implemented a lot of the steps, but still have a long way to go.

Upon winning the battle within, the next step in your journey is becoming responsible toward reality. There is so much for you to gain in the next section; head over there now for additional insight.

Chapter Nine

Being Responsible Toward Reality

In life, there are two facets to living; what we desire and what is real.

What we desire resides in our minds, it is a complete make-up of thoughts and ideas that we reach for daily in the quest to become better. For example, you may desire a Ferrari because it is a great car that shows elegance.

However, the reality of the situation is that you may not be able to afford a Ferrari. That means there is often a gap between desire and reality. What we want is not always want we can get and what we can get may not be what we desire.

This concept plays a significant role in the attainment of self-esteem, because for some people, their inability to get the things they desire makes them feel inadequate. This affects their self-esteem negatively.

In this chapter, we will consider the ways in which you can become responsible for reality. So clearly, the focus isn't just on our desires, because desires can be very misleading.

Before we get to the practical aspects of this chapter, I want you to understand how desires work. Desires spring upon us; they are like fantasies, wishes, and ideas we get that inspire a need within us.

You can be walking down the street and pass by an ice-cream shop; suddenly you want to get ice-cream. Now, before you saw the shop, there was no craving for ice-cream or anything cold. So what makes you want it so badly that you spend money getting it immediately? It's DESIRE!

When desire is left uncontrolled, it can lead to dire consequences and a constant battle with your reality. The goal for anyone who wants to improve self-esteem should be to welcome desires - but know when to indulge such feelings and when not to.

Back to the connection this has with self-esteem. If you are unable to buy the ice-cream at the time and also unable to purchase several other things you desire consecutively, it will have a significant impact on your self-esteem.

You start to feel like you are being deprived of things others enjoy. The more you think that way, the worse you feel about yourself - and then you start to lose confidence.

The solution to all of these is simple; be responsible enough to know what YOUR REALITY is and stick to it. Remember that your reality may be different from that of your friend who may be able to afford all of his desires.

The concept of desire isn't restricted to just items you can buy, but the experiences and skills you want to enjoy. There are times you may have to take a break from certain activities, and in those times, you must never allow the feeling of not doing these things to affect your self-esteem.

Once you embrace your reality, life becomes less complicated. You no longer feel pressured to do things because other people are doing them. Instead, you are comfortable with where you are currently, knowing that your desires may not be fulfilled instantly but will be eventually.

Now, that's another thought process for you to explore. If you realise that you will get every good thing you deserve eventually, you will not be in a hurry to accomplish all you want immediately.

When you are responsible for your reality, you will be taking the pressure off of yourself to impress others and alter what you can do. Now that you have an understanding of how desire and reality connect, the next step should be how you can become responsible for your reality. So here goes:

How to be Accountable for the Truth

1. Be Content
When you are content with what you have, it becomes easier for you to be responsible for your reality. Appreciate where you are as you reach for more, but be satisfied with the process.

Contentment makes it possible for you to stick to only what your reality can afford. As such, you tend to be happy with your decisions and still keep your self-esteem intact.

Always make decisions from a place of contentment. It is a pathway to ensuring a good life, especially if you are keen on building solid self-esteem.

2. Take Charge of Your Desires
Your desires shouldn't have rule over you at any time. Always take charge of how you feel and be in control of what you choose to do and what you choose not to do.

Instead of being carried away by your desires, build resistance within yourself by sticking to what is essential. One of the most vital signs of a person who has got great self-esteem is the ability to stay in charge regardless of what happens around them.

3. Build Resistance
For you to be responsible for your reality, it is essential that you build strength against some things early enough. You know, those things

that affect you personally and cause you to stick to desires over reality; develop a healthy mindset against them.

Some people are described as being strong-willed. Such a description speaks of someone who is not easily moved by anything. So regardless of what you come across, you maintain the same disposition, and this is how you build very stable self-esteem.

4. **Be Surrounded by Like-Minds**
If a person who is shopaholic hangs around others like them, they will never change. So, if you spend time with people who cannot be responsible for their reality, you will also become a victim of your desires.

While you work on yourself and your self-esteem, do not forget or neglect the power of people. Anyone you are close to wields considerable influence over your life (positively or negatively).

Until you become mindful of the kind of people you spend time with, you will not be able to distinguish between desires and reality.

5. **Plan, Plan, Plan**
When you don't plan, you automatically set yourself up for problems. You can completely eradicate the issues that pop up with desires and reality just by planning carefully.

Plan for everything you want to do or purchase and after that, ensure that you stick to the program. So, if you already have a plan of what to do about the items you want to shop for, there will be minimal or no desires to reach for what isn't in your plan.

With planning, you can build and maintain a stable lifestyle that doesn't cause you to experience low self-esteem or dissatisfaction with yourself over your inability to get what you want.

6. **Learn the Art of Compromise**
Sometimes, all you need to do is compromise a little to get the desired results. Come on! Life is about compromise, especially when it is done for the greater good.

You may have to let go of something irrelevant (your desires) for something even better (your reality). When you start to compromise, you will begin to understand how things play out effortlessly with the right strategies.

With compromise, you will most certainly be giving up the worse option for the best and the more often you do this, the higher your chances of building stronger self-esteem.

7. **Substitute Your Desires**
At other times, all you must do is substitute your desires. For example, if you cannot get the Ferrari you want, what other vehicle can you use that will give you the same feeling of satisfaction the Ferrari offers?

It is all about being happy at the end of the day, and one of the fastest ways to become satisfied as you love yourself and improve on your self-esteem is by knowing when to substitute an item or experience that doesn't fit into your reality.

Substituted desire also means you get to satisfy your hunger for more, but in the most comfortable way. In the end, you will be happy for the substitution.

8. **Set Goals**
Goals are like plans. They are the ideas you have before setting the program in motion. So, with goals, it becomes possible for you to streamline what you want and stick to it.

As you set goals for yourself, you will be training your mind to get used to the process of planning, thus eliminating spontaneous impulses that encourage irresponsibility toward your reality.

You can build self-esteem that isn't affected by petty things just by being responsible and deliberate about accepting your reality. Go for what you want after you have calculated the risks and mapped out strategies on how you can keep your high self-esteem intact while making individual decisions.

Aside from being in touch with your reality, you have to also embrace the concept of learning consistently because that is a crucial ingredient for building great self-esteem. Learning never ends; get set to learn some more as you head over to the next section now.

Chapter Ten

A Commitment to Learning Always

Building self-esteem is a process. Sometimes it is a lifelong endeavour that doesn't have an end. If you are committed to it, you will always have something new to spice things up. Some people climb up the ladder, cultivate very good self-esteem, and yet they are unable to sustain it for the long haul.

We will address the issue of sustenance in another chapter, but before we get there, you should know that for you to attain heights with self-esteem and continue with it, they must be willing to take on the path of learning.

What are you doing right now? You are reading through material that is instrumental in helping you become a man who is fearless, daring, and ready to achieve big things. By reading this book, you have shown your desire to learn; but it doesn't end with one book.

Now that you know some of the principles of building self-esteem, you need to become even more committed to learning, because life is very dynamic. The people you meet, the places you go, and the experiences you have all affect your self-esteem at some point.

So, for you to continue the path you have set for yourself and the precedence you have set with this book, there is a need for continuous learning and growth.

The books you will read five years from now, and the podcasts and messages you will listen to in the future about self-esteem will contain a different word. Because there will be a lot of changes in your life then, you will also have to adopt new measures.

Anyone who has ever succeeded at anything will tell you that the educational and growth process never ends. You start it, and then you have a responsibility to uphold the process by going for more knowledge.

When something is important to you, you create time to work at it until you achieve your goals. So how important is this self-esteem issue to you? Are you willing to make it a major priority in your life? Are there steps required of you that you have made? Do you reach out for more?

The answers to the questions above will determine if you will continue with this chapter. Well, if you are ready to take on the process by learning continually, ensure that you take the tips you will find below seriously.

How to Improve Your Commitment to Learning

1. Read Books
The wisdom and knowledge of this world is found in books. If you aren't reading, you are dying. All religious sects in the world have their laws and rules contained in a "Holy book," because books are a symbol of true wisdom.

If you are going to learn more about self-esteem, you will need to read books about the subject matter — thumbs-up to you for reading one now, but don't allow this to be the last one. So off you go to the library and bookshops as you take your time searching for books about self-esteem.

Aside from physical copies of books, you should also get e-books that can be downloaded on your mobile phone, so you can read on the go. Subscribe to magazines that handle issues around self-esteem and you will be glad you did.

2. Listen to Podcasts on the Go

There are numerous podcasts on self-esteem. The most inspiring thing about podcasts is the fact that you can listen from anywhere in the world.

As you listen, you will feel a distinct connection to the speaker that makes it seem as if you are sitting right next to them as they admonish you on building self-esteem.

Podcasts are becoming very popular these days, especially in a world where technology is the most viable tool. What are you waiting for? Get your data-enabled phone, laptop, or mobile device and download podcasts you can listen to today as you make progress with your self-esteem.

3. Read Biographies of Great People

The most successful people in the world also have stories of how they overcame their self-esteem challenges. One very productive way of learning is by reading through their biographies to discover some of the steps they took in becoming more confident.

As you read through biographies, you will discover patterns among these great people and gain insight into how they shattered expectations just by believing in themselves.

If you have never read a biography before, today is a good day to read about someone who inspires you. Learning about other people is a sustainable means of maintaining all the lessons you have gleaned thus far.

4. Utilize Search Engines

Search engines such as Google are an excellent platform for learning. You can research anything and learn how to build confidence. Search engines offer a wide range of options when it comes to knowledge.

By just typing "How to improve my self-esteem," you will be exposed to a myriad of options, steps, tips, and lessons that will inspire you to take the right steps and do the right things to ensure maximum results.

A search engine is what is standing between you and what you don't know. Use it today and take your learning further.

5.   Listen to Others Share Their Stories
There are people around you who have experienced their own self-esteem journeys. By listening to them, you will learn lessons and pick out one or two tips that will inspire your trip.

So, learn to pay attention to others, and you can get people to share their unique stories by also sharing yours. Whenever you get an opportunity to converse with someone, talk about self-love or confidence - something that will encourage them to also share their experiences.

As you listen to others share, you will be inspired to take the right steps.

6.   Join a Self-Esteem Group or Create One
If there are little groups on your street or in your office that comprise people coming around to share their experiences, join and contribute as you also listen to others.

However, if there are no self-esteem groups around you, create one! With all you have gained from this book, you can organize a reading club where you can share the content of this book with other men.

At such reading clubs, people should be given an opportunity to share their unique experiences; through this method, everyone learns, and everyone gains something from each other, as well.

7. Follow Self-Esteem Coaches on Social Media

Numerous coaches on social media can help you improve your self-esteem. If you are an avid social media user, all you need to do is search for such coaches and follow them.

Some of their tweets, posts, and videos are free. You can comment on their pages and get instant responses while interacting with other followers and users who want to improve their self-esteem as well. Through social media, there is so much a person can learn if willing.

Don't waste the opportunity by being complacent.

8. Learn from Your Mistakes

A mistake is a sign that you are trying. The best thing you can do is learn from your mistakes, make the resolution to be better, and refuse to hold yourself back because of them.

The learning process entails you sometimes going overboard with plans or not even doing anything at all. Whatever the case will be, ensure that you are always learning from the things you fail at.

With a mindset to learn, you will view mistakes as opportunities to improve. Remember that improving one's self-esteem is a life-long process. It gets better gradually; it does not happen in one day. The more mistakes you make, the closer you get to your goal.

9. Subscribe to a Mailing List

If you subscribe to a mailing list sent by an expert on self-esteem issues, you will have an opportunity to learn from that person periodically. Mailing lists are also excellent because they offer a unique chance to get first-hand information from self-esteem professionals.

With every email you get, digest the content and add value to your experience by reading and learning. You can also share what you have learned with others; this will make the lessons stick with you for a longer period of time.

10. Get a Mentor

Everyone needs a mentor!

At this stage of your journey, you need a mentor who will hold your hand and guide you through this process. Your mentor should be someone who has also had the same self-esteem experience and overcome it graciously.

If you find such a person, reach out to them and you never know, you might get a great mentor who is willing to help you. As a mentee, you have a responsibility to listen to your mentor, ask questions, and follow through with everything you are taught.

Mentorship is a sure way to continue learning and to improve on all you have gained thus far.

Education is one aspect of life that never ends; you start learning from the day you were born and it doesn't stop until you die. So, make your self-esteem journey have the same lifelong process as you implement all you have discovered in this chapter.

Did you know that addictions have a firm hold on how you feel about yourself? The next section seeks to elucidate on how habits affect self-esteem; there are so many other ideas to be shared in that section, so head over there now and get started.

Chapter Eleven

Kicking Addictions Out

Addiction is the primary cause of low self-esteem. If you have ever been addicted to something before now, you should know that one of the reasons why you struggled with the addiction is because you weren't confident in yourself and your ability to overcome the challenge.

Addictions usually start as habits. At first, they may even seem like simple indulgences that don't affect you, but gradually they begin to get the best of you and take over your life.

There are two things we must consider when placing addiction and self-esteem side by side. First, some people become addicted to certain things because of low self-esteem. Second, some escape addiction and battle with low self-esteem.

There has been a recognized relationship between self-esteem and addiction for decades. Drug users were found to have low self-esteem, and this explains why they rely on the effects of drugs to stimulate a temporary sense of confidence.

People who are addicted to the Internet, eating, compulsive buying, and even pornography all suffer from low self-esteem. When they indulge in their addictions, their insecurities are masked, and they enjoy short-lived feelings of confidence. This shrinks their self-esteem even more in the long term.

So in the end, addictions are a terrible influence on your self-esteem. This chapter is an efficient one; you will read through steps and tips on how you can avoid both self-esteem pitfalls concerning addictions.

First, we will consider how to avoid getting addicted as a result of low self-esteem. Then, we will discuss how to build self-esteem after an addiction. By the time we get to the end of this chapter, you will be a brand-new man who is ready with a clean slate.

Now, if you are reading and you have never had any experiences with addiction, you might feel like you want to pass on this chapter, but I want you to hold it right there for a moment.

You may not be dealing with addiction right now, but you may know someone who is fighting to be free from it. Remember that you are not only reading for yourself; you are reading and learning to make an impact in the lives of others as well.

So, if you have issues with addiction, read on. And if you don't have problems with addiction, read so you can lift someone else up. We will begin with the first phase of the journey to getting free of addiction so low self-esteem can be a topic of the past.

How to Avoid the Pitfall of Addiction from Low Self-Esteem

1. Focus on Yourself
When you discover that you are getting close to becoming addicted to something, try to focus on yourself even more. Some people will instead spend time with the material or event that leads them to full-blown addiction - and this is where the problem starts.

By paying attention to yourself, you will be able to deduce why you are feeling less confident - thus handling the issue from the moment it begins.

2. Find the Causes of the Problem

Now that you have total focus on yourself, you need also to discover the cause of the problem. Why are you feeling this way? Why is your self-esteem at an all-time low? When you are determined to find answers, you will figure out the challenge.

The cause of the problem will most likely be something that makes you uncomfortable, so analyse your life and fish out those things that make you unhappy or uncomfortable; this is where the problem lies.

3. Talk to Someone

Don't wait until you start indulging in the addiction before you speak with someone who can help. A drowning man calls out for help, so reach out to someone who can help you at this phase before it's too late.

When you speak with someone, you will be able to share your burden, have a shoulder to lean on, and get advice as well.

4. Avoid Spending Time Alone

In times like this, you shouldn't waste time alone. Be surrounded by people, friends, and family who want the best for you. When you isolate yourself, the thoughts of addiction are reinforced, and this can pose a significant problem for you.

So, get out of the house, hang out with your dearest pals, and build meaningful relationships that will serve as a guiding light for you in times like this.

5. Start Rebuilding Confidence

More than ever, now is the time to start rebuilding your confidence level. Don't allow negative thoughts to get through to your head. Indulge in good, healthy activities and always protect your mind.

Gradually, you will regain your confidence and put this unpleasant phase behind you for good.

How to Build Self-Esteem after an Addiction

1. Write out Affirmations

Again, affirmations are very useful in helping you rebuild your self-esteem. Tell yourself how proud you are of all you have accomplished, and continue to speak positive words to yourself so you are encouraged to do even better.

You can write out your affirmations and place them close to where you can read them out easily every day.

2. Forgive Yourself

People who have struggled with addiction are plagued with self-blame and guilt-trip themselves, thus making it difficult for them to forgive their errors. Now isn't the time to beat yourself up over what happened in the past.

Acknowledge that what you did was wrong and then move on from the issue by committing to doing things differently. Your past failures should not define your present.

3. Accept Compliments

When a person suffers from low self-esteem, they will be very quick to dismiss a tribute, but now that you are trying to rebuild your self-esteem, accept compliments graciously.

Smile at the person giving the compliment and ensure that you also say something nice to him/her. Accepting compliments is an easy way of bringing a lot of good into your life.

4. Do Something Kind Every Day

Kindness is therapeutic; you can increase the appreciation that others express toward you by being kind to them. Now, consideration doesn't have to be something grand or huge. By doing straightforward things, you can make someone else feel good, thus putting a smile on your own face.

You can also volunteer to help others in need as a way of rebuilding your self-esteem. If you are kind, the universe and other people will be kind to you as well.

5. Make the Necessary Changes

As you do something kind, be mindful of the fact that you will have to start making meaningful changes in your lifestyle immediately. First, you should avoid the places you used to go that weren't good for you.

You know the peculiarities of your addiction so try to put a stop to everything that will lead you back to where you were before now.

6. Get Rid of Addictive Materials

As you make the necessary changes, you should also get free of all addictive substances that will take you back to the life you are trying to escape. So videotapes, credit cards, drugs, etc. that are unhealthy for you should be thrown away.

With the addictive materials out of the way, you will be able to create an enabling environment for your new lifestyle to blossom. Go through your items and remove all traces of materials that will take you back.

7. Speak to a Therapist

A therapist is always a good idea, especially when you need to get out of severe addiction. A therapist is a third-party who will be objective in their analysis of your situation. Be open to listening and gaining insight into how you can get out of addiction.

8. Take Baby Steps

You won't get out of the habit in a flash so be ready to start by taking baby steps. Remember that it took you a while to get here, so it will take a while to get out of it as well.

Everything you decide to do to change must be handled with care; if you try to rush the process of getting out of addiction, you will fall right back into it. So, exercise patience by taking baby steps.

9. Be Patient with the Process

The fact that you have decided to change doesn't mean it is going to happen all at once. There is a process, and you must be patient with it; your ability to stay patient through it all will determine how far you go with the change.

There will be times when it seems like you might relapse; hold on tight and believe the best about yourself.

10. Love is All That Matters

When you love yourself enough, you will surely want to protect yourself from anything that is harmful to your mental, emotional, and psychological space. After getting over an addiction, what you should do is fill your mind with self-love.

Love yourself and appreciate life; it is the only way you can solidify all you have learned here. With love, you can overcome every obstacle that comes your way. Remember also to love others; it is your way of extending a hand of kindness to them.

Your life can be so much better despite addiction, but you must be willing to put up a fight for what you want. If you are not doing anything to kick the addiction out, you will continue to wallow in it.

The message of this chapter is two-fold:

1. If you are at a shallow place in your life right now, do not turn to addiction.

2. If you were able to get out of the habit, rebuild your self-esteem and maintain a clean slate with life afterward.

If you can internalize both messages, you will be on your way to a better life, free from addiction and the problems it presents. We have been going on and on about you for a while now. It is time to consider the relationships you have with other people and how they shape your self-esteem. Head over to the next chapter and read through the ideas you will find there.

Chapter Twelve

How do you treat others?

They say the way you treat others is a reflection of who you are. People with low self-esteem often treat others around them poorly because they are unhappy with themselves. So if you are going to enjoy high self-esteem, you will have to seek out ways of ensuring that you treat people well.

As simple as the opening paragraph is, so many people still fall victim to the trap of being nasty to others such that at the end of the day, they are alone because no one wants to be friends with people who aren't nice.

Well, when you stay alone long enough, you start to feel isolated, and this affects the quality of the relationships you enjoy with others. Loneliness is a breeding ground for very low self-esteem, and just like that, you find yourself having problems.

As a man who is keen on becoming an Alpha male, it is crucial that you treat others around you the same way you will want to be treated. This is a trait those with high self-esteem portray; they view everyone as equal and try to leave a lasting impression on the minds of others.

So at the end of the day, people who are friendly, kind, and giving to others can build a support system for themselves. They hear a lot of kind words as well and have a rich deposit of self-confidence.

I want you to take some time to ask yourself this all-important question; do I treat other people well? Am I a kind person? Do people leave me feeling inspired? Or am I rude and abusive? A portion of the Holy book that Christians read states that "Out of the abundance of the heart, the mouth speaks." You will only say to others what you've got on the onside.

If you are filled with a lot of hate, anger, and bitterness, you will never be kind to others, and this will gradually erode you of whatever self-esteem you've got left. This chapter isn't about you (we have been going on and on about you since we started). This chapter tries to strike a balance between what you can do to improve your self-esteem and your connections with other people.

When it comes to treating other people well, you must be deliberate about it. Being intentional with the relationships you build will cause you to appreciate the link you've got with yourself, as well. We are going to get right to the tips you can implement that will help you treat other people well enough to give your self-esteem the boost it deserves.

How to Treat Other People Well for High Self-Esteem

1. Be Conscious of Others
As a person who is trying to build high self-esteem, you must become aware of others. You are not an island on your own; you coexist with people around you. As such, it is essential you take into consideration their likes, dislikes, and everything else that is important to them.

When you become conscious of others, you will also discover ways through which you can be useful to them.

Start with the people around you; your home offices, out on the streets, etc., reach out to someone with a smile and make a difference just by being aware of the people around you.

2. Random Acts of Kindness

Random acts of kindness refer to the process of being friendly and kind-hearted towards people you don't even know. You could pay for a stranger's transport fare or provide food and shelter for orphans.

Only a person who is satisfied and happy with his own life will attempt helping people he doesn't know. So, you get to see the connection between being kind and self-esteem.

Random acts of kindness can also take the form of doing nice things for those you love unexpectedly. How about showing up at your friend's house with pastries and cookies on Christmas morning? You can be the most beautiful, self-accepting person ever; all you must do is start being kind to others one person at a time.

3. Listen More Than You Speak

If you pay attention to what people are saying more than you talk to them, you will discover new things about them. The person who listens receives information that is instrumental in helping him make a difference in the life of another person.

Now that you have started building self-esteem, you must become consumed with the idea of giving more of yourself in service to others. Being a good listener will help you live a very impactful life; it is a testament to how far you have come in developing your self-esteem.

4. Show Respect to All

One of the best ways to show people you care is by being respectful to them. There is a famous saying that respect is reciprocal; and this is so true. People will only show you respect when they perceive that you are respectful to them, as well.

Show respect by honouring other people's decisions. Try not to force your ideas on others and appreciate the efforts they make every day to live well. Little words such as "Thank you," "I am sorry," or "Good morning," go a very long way showing how respectful you are toward others.

5. Accept People for Who They Are
Instead of trying to change others and make them into what you've envisaged in your head, try to be accommodating and accept them for who they are.

Everyone won't be the same, we all won't like or want the same things - and that is okay. When you meet someone who loves what you like, great! However, when you come across a person who is entirely different from you in all aspects, learn to tolerate them and work with them just as they are. Accepting people for who they are is a sign of high self-esteem.

6. Follow the Golden Rule
What does the "golden control" state? "Do to others as you would want them to do to you". Whatever you want everyone else to do to you, start doing it to other people as well.

If you want people to smile at you, smile more often, and if you want people to share with you, go right ahead and share with others, too. If you are committed to the happiness of others, someone else or a group of people will also be committed to your happiness.

Write the golden rule plainly so you can see it and scan it. It will serve as a constant reminder that you have an obligation towards others that must be fulfilled.

7. Don't Pull People Down
This is so important! In a bid to rise to the top, too many people try to pull others down. Your light will not shine more brightly because someone else's view is dim.

Remember that we rise by lifting others.

More so, you will be affecting the self-esteem of the person you are pulling down, so it will be a case of hurting someone with something you are trying to avoid.

When you make it your lifelong mission to help everyone you meet, you won't have to think about pulling someone else down so you can rise.

8. Don't Look Down on Anyone
You may not be on the same level as everyone else, but it isn't a reason for you to look down on those who are not on the high level you perceive yourself to be on.

In the next chapter you will read about humility, and you will discover the reason why it is so essential for you to consider everyone as being equal.

The moment you start to look down on others, your self-esteem begins to diminish. Preserve all you have worked so hard for by treating everyone with fairness, dignity, respect, and love.

9. Be Gracious to All
When we speak of being polite, we refer to being incredibly kind, merciful, and compassionate towards other. A lot of people do not know how to be courteous, so they skip this step. But this one is important.

It is good to be kind, but it is better to be gracious. Being kind is something you do while being conscious; you plan for it, and it happens as you have envisioned.

Being gracious is something you do even when you don't feel like it. You go out of your way to make things happen for other people, and that is one of the hallmarks of being a man with high self-esteem.

10. Appreciate Those Who Support You

There will always be those who are your support system in life; these people cheer you on and are huge pillars you can lean on at any time. As such, you should celebrate them by showing appreciation for all they've done for you.

According to a recent study, people who do not express gratitude to those who have done well for them suffer from very low self-esteem. You are different, so it is essential that you appreciate those who hold your hand through the crises and problems you face in life.

If treating people nicely is a prerequisite for you to enjoy the best of self-esteem, then I suggest that you take it seriously. You will only feel as good as you make others feel. When people speak of how well you treat them, it is an opportunity for you to pat yourself on the back.

Now, the fact that you are determined to help others and treat them well doesn't mean everyone will be helpful to you, as well. Come on, it is a cold world after all. But regardless of how you are treated, you must insist on taking this path and not looking back.

You shouldn't be kind to others because they are helpful to you; be generous because it is your nature to be that way. People with very high self-esteem go out of their way to make things happen for others. Another trait of a person with high self-esteem is humility; the next chapter does justice to this feature.

Chapter Thirteen

Humility is a Tool

We have been on such a fantastic ride from the very first chapter until now, and it gets better and better with each section. Now we are going to consider a vital tool needed in giving your self-esteem a significant boost; and that tool is Humility.

Everyone wants to be associated with humble people who make them feel special. Come on, ordinary people are just the best, aren't they? So why not be the humble person who makes other people feel excited? It is quite rare to find people with very high self-esteem who are rude and proud.

Good self-esteem is a product of a mind that has accepted all of its flaws and imperfections and still thinks he is fantastic. There is a feeling of humility that comes with being able to say, "Oh, I know I am not perfect, but I am on my way to greater things."

If you are always humble, you will not struggle with maintaining high self-esteem; it will become a lifestyle for you. But humility must be practiced; it must be groomed and nurtured over time for it to be sustained. More importantly, as a humble person, you will be able to influence others as well.

As opposed to popular opinion, humility is not a sign of low self-esteem. People can be very humble yet exhibit a high sense of appreciation for who they are and the journey they have been on.

I want you to think about humility and self-esteem from two perspectives. First, you can utilize humility as a tool to build self-esteem, and second, you can use it to gain power over people.

So, what you should be concerned with in this chapter is how to use humility as a tool for the advancement of your self-esteem. You must have observed that almost every section in this book contains steps, tips, and ideas. Well, the reason for the levels is for you to have something you can hold on to even after reading the book.

I can come here and write an epistle. I can go on and on about how you can be humble. But, if I don't show you the steps to take, it will all be a waste of time. So once again, I request your indulgence as you read through steps you can take toward using humility to build higher self-esteem.

With these steps, you will be required to take action immediately as you learn them. After every tip, there is an accountability step that ensures you utilize the step.

How to Build Higher Self-Esteem through Humility

1. Be Available for People
Humility is about putting yourself aside for others, sometimes. The best way to show that you care for someone is by being available for them.

Sometimes we pride ourselves in being so busy that we forget the importance of being a pillar of strength someone can lean on in difficult times. It takes a person with healthy self-esteem to be there for someone else despite having their challenges.

Your friends and family members, as well as strangers, should say that you are a reliable person - someone they can count on at any time.

Accountability Task: Go through your messages and chats with friends, discover who is experiencing a tough time right now, and create time in your schedule to be there for them.

When you show up for that person, don't make the entire situation about you; the more you do this for others, the better you will feel about yourself.

2. Avoid Baseless Arguments

Arguments are good. In fact, most intellectual conversations stem from arguments. But, baseless arguments are a complete waste of time. Whenever you find yourself in a gathering where people shout and scream to prove their point, get out of there.

Humility is all about positivity. If you are going to have a conversation with someone that isn't positive, then you must start to consider bringing that conversation to an end.

Baseless arguments will also make you think less of yourself, especially when you are struggling with the idea of building a very firm, strong self-esteem. Be smart enough to know when to let go of a discussion.

Accountability Task: The next time you go out with friends and colleagues, be mindful of the kind of conversations you engage in with them. Once the discussion starts to go south, that is the signal for you to take your leave.

3. Admit when You are Wrong

When you meet a person who is unable to admit their wrongs, you have just reached a proud person. We haven't come this far to be proud now, have we? So, you are going to kick that feeling out by admitting to your wrongs.

People with low self-esteem will always want to insist on being right, regardless of how glaring their fault is. Be a noble person by accepting your wrongs and doing your best to become a better person.

Accountability Task: The next time you do something wrong, admit to it and learn your lesson. If you weren't aware that you made a wrong move, when others point it out to you, try not to be defensive. Life is not about being right all the time; it is about growing and learning.

4. **Be a Cheerleader**
We love cheerleaders because they add colour and fun to the game. But in life, cheerleaders do more than that. Cheerleaders in real life don't get to wear costumes; they are our most significant support systems which will take our hands when we are faced with a challenge and help us walk through it with confidence.

The point is this; you have to be a cheerleader to someone else. Now the person might be a subordinate, but they will be grateful for the help you render. Cheer your partners on; clap and celebrate with your friends when they reach a milestone.

With cheerleading in life, it isn't about who is winning; it is all about being there for anyone who wins.

Accountability task: You have got to have someone you cheer on currently. Look within your inner circle and search for that person who is embarking on a project and needs a little help. Remember that you reflect how you make people feel.

5. **Help Others Become Better**
As you cheer others on, make sure you are taking steps toward making them feel better, as well. It is so easy for us to become self-

absorbed and think about ourselves. After all, we are all that matters right? But this shouldn't be the case.

Your ability to reach out to someone with an idea or skill that will help them is one of the hallmarks of humility. People continually seek better ways of doing things through collaborations, so who are you working with now? How can you make that best friend of yours extremely good at what they do?

By always thinking about others, you will be helping yourself, as well.

Accountability Task: Think about something you can do for someone that will add value to their experience. It doesn't have to be something big; most times the smallest gestures mean the most to others.

6. **Give People Credit**
In a bid to be harsh, we often withhold credit when it is due for others, and this is wrong. If you are a leader in your sector, it is okay for you to be stern when you need to be - but also give credit to others when it is due.

How would you feel knowing that you have done a great job and your boss doesn't even acknowledge it? Oh, I bet you would feel so terrible that it might affect your self-esteem.

If you don't want to work with people who have low self-esteem, make sure you give them credit when it is due. Also, if you're going to enjoy very high self-esteem continually, you must be kind to other people. It is a way of extending kindness to yourself, as well.

Accountability Task: Reward excellence the next time someone does something remarkable for you.

7. Don't Compare People

It can all be fun and games when you compare Mr. A with Mr. B, but trust me when I say it isn't right. The art of putting two people side by side doesn't showcase humility. Nor does it make you a better person.

Always remember that people are different. Your ability to accept them for who they are is what makes you stand out and aids in maintaining better relationships with others.

Be the man who walks into a room and can reach out to everyone, regardless of their flaws. Be a friend to all and a man of great character; humility will make you stand out.

Accountability Task: Appreciate the goodness in other people by looking out for their great traits and not their flaws. Let each one you know be an original and not a duplicate of another person. Be kind with your words and avoid the pitfalls of comparison.

8. Be Teachable

Have you observed that people who are not teachable are often very proud? Oh yes, they are! When a person becomes unteachable, they also find it difficult to build good self-esteem. You must make up your mind to be someone who can make changes at any time.

By being teachable, we are referring to the art of being an avid learner who has an open mind toward life. You are not stereotyped; neither should you insist on having your way all the time.

A person with high self-esteem realizes that they can learn from other people in the same way they can teach others.

Accountability Task: Make up your mind to learn something new. Seek out someone who can teach you, and regardless of the person's social status, be open to learning and adding more to your knowledge.

9. Volunteer

It is always a good time to give to others. Therefore, volunteering is crucial. You can show how humble you are by reaching out to people you don't know and people who may never have enough to pay you back.

There are multiple opportunities through which you can volunteer: homeless shelters, orphanages, old people's homes, etc. Seek out the organization you like and do something special for them.

You will be amazed at how great you feel every time you volunteer to help others. This process also aids in building better self-esteem; so keep at it for the long haul.

Accountability task: Make a list of all the non-profit organizations you know. From that list, create a plan that entails you paying a visit to one of the groups at least once a month. Ensure that you stick to your plans monthly, weekly or yearly (it depends on what works best for you).

Humility is not just about being modest; it is all about being able to handle yourself in a classy way and still make an impact on the lives of others. What we have achieved with this chapter is teaching you some of the most effective steps you can take toward building self-esteem through a humble mindset.

As we wrap up this chapter, please be reminded that HUMILITY IS POWER UNDER CONTROL.

You've got all the power, yet you can put others first; that is what humility is all about. We spoke briefly about falling in love with yourself a while back; let's take it a step further as we analyse more about that concept in the next chapter.

Chapter Fourteen

Falling in Love with Yourself

We spoke about this briefly in the previous section, but it is just too important to only get a brief mention. Self-esteem is all about love! We cannot talk about building self-esteem without talking about how much we should love ourselves and others.

Love is a significant ingredient needed to build up one's self-esteem and sustain it long term (we will consider the steps you should take toward sustainability in the last chapter, look forward to reading that).

So, for you to grow and improve your self-esteem, you have to first love yourself. The extent to which you love yourself determines how you will love others, as well. You cannot give what you don't have. As such, you can only express love to people from the abundance of love you feel for yourself.

How well you love yourself will also go a long way in showing how patient you will be with others. A person who loves themselves will do everything within their power to be happy! Happy people are individuals with amazing self-esteem; they are so satisfied with their lives that they are not willing to allow negative feelings into their minds.

How do you know you love yourself? What are the indicators that show how much you appreciate who you are? If you were going to recommend yourself as a friend to someone, would you say you are a great person? Questions like these should put a lot of things into perspective for you.

Love is about acceptance.

Love is about embracing all of who you are.

Love is the feeling of content

Love is being committed to one's happiness.

Love is patient.

Love is about kindness.

Love is high self-esteem.

If you are not sure about the love you have for yourself, I want you to carry out a brief exercise before we go on. Get your journal and write down ten things you love about yourself. The ten things can cut across skills, abilities, and behavioural patterns.

After writing, read these traits out loud to yourself and reaffirm that you have got the present in your life for good. If you are honest with yourself, you will realize that indeed there is so much about you that is good and worthy of celebration.

With self-love, you don't have to wait for someone else to tell you how special you are. Self-love is like a spring that bursts forth from within you and sprinkles life, hope, and more love into every area of your life. You have to turn on the faucet of this spring by first recognizing all the great qualities you've got on the inside.

No one is a complete flop; there may be a time when it seems like you don't have it all together, but if you embrace your truth, you will realize that you are a superstar who has a few bumps once in a while.

In this chapter, you are going to come across the top ten principles of self-love and discover how you can use these principles in your own life. The key to getting the best out of these steps is simple; READ, UNDERSTAND, ACT, AND DON'T STOP ACTING! I can't wait for us to get to the chapter on sustenance, so let's wrap this up quickly because the last section is already upon us.

Principles of Self-love for Better Self-Esteem

1. The Law of Self-Compassion
Self-love can only become fully manifested when you are compassionate toward yourself. This principle is akin to being conscious of what your weaknesses are and still loving who you are regardless.

You can practice compassion through patience; when you fall off the path you have crafted for yourself, pick yourself up and move on purposefully. Compassionate people are known to be kind, as well. It is safe to say that this principle urges you to be kind.

Whenever you feel tempted to be hard on yourself, remember that you are on this journey of self-love and it is imperative to show compassion toward yourself.

2. The Principle of Being Responsible
Self-love will not be easily accomplished when you are irresponsible with your life. A responsible person shows that they have regard for their life, so they make very wise choices that guide them through their journey.

Being responsible isn't a trait you can negotiate or do without. You have got to show an excellent example by examining the life choices you make and ensuring that these choices align with the greater vision you have for your life.

Don't do things that hurt yourself; self-love is tender and gentle. Be committed to living responsibly today as you take time off daily to analyse the choices you make and how they affect you long term.

3. The Principle of Being Non-Judgemental of Yourself
In a bid to be excellent, you will want to be highly critical, and this will lead to being judgemental. Love doesn't pass judgment even in worst-case scenarios. Avoid being too hard on yourself and trust that you are on the right path regardless of the challenges you face.

Being non-judgemental also pushes you to accept yourself, know your strengths, and strategize on how to work on your weaknesses. Even when you are angered by your actions and inactions, don't judge yourself.

Always remember that you are the captain of this ship and you must be in charge, leading with love and self-acceptance.

4. The Principle of Patience
We cannot talk about self-love without patience. Some people give up on themselves because they aren't patient enough to see all their efforts come to fruition. Being patient doesn't mean you tolerate bad behaviour, it means you get to appreciate where you are now while hoping for the best to come.

Love and patience go together; you cannot love without being patient, and you cannot be patient if you don't love. As you focus on building high self-esteem, be determined to be patient with yourself on this journey and take into consideration the areas you can improve upon.

5. The Principle of Quiet Acceptance
This principle speaks of a person accepting themselves as they are. It is often easy to take yourself for granted, especially when you feel

like you can be more. Love will make you admit who you are because love is about faith.

Don't wait for someone else to give you approval or offer you a commendation for being a good person. Remember that this journey is all about your personality, so you've got to take responsibility for it.

When you come to a place of acceptance, you also let go of fear. You investigate the future with hope knowing that you are enough.

6. The Principle of Faith in the Unknown

The reason some people start to feel a sense of low self-esteem is that they are sceptical about the future. So, they wake up every day in panic mode, thinking about how their tomorrow will turn out and how they will get the best out of their day.

Well, if you continue to be apprehensive about the future, you will probably never learn to love yourself. It is okay to wonder what will happen next, but it is not alright for you to WORRY about it.

Love is about embracing today and having faith in a future that may be unknown. By being sceptical, you may draw yourself back into the shell of low self-esteem. So be bold about tomorrow, because love conquers all things - even the future.

7. The Principle of Being Authentic

Through it all, remember that you are an original and not a copy of someone else. You must follow through with the policy of being genuine and real.

Love is about embracing all of you and being real about it. The best way to love anyone is to accept them for who they are; but the best way to enjoy yourself is by being authentic with your story.

Don't try to be like someone else; don't try to take snippets of another man's life and add to yours. You are already on your way to a more magnificent journey of self-esteem, so don't ruin it by being unsure of who you are.

8. The Principle of Love and Health
Self-love will not work out for anyone who isn't mindful of health. Come on, would you be reading this book if you were unhealthy? Would you be able to implement all these principles if you were in the hospital?
They say, "Health is wealth," but I say health is EVERYTHING!

The ideas behind self-love will only be what they are – ideas. Until you start working on them from a position of good health, you will not enjoy the process. To adhere to this principle, make sure you are full of health enough to love yourself unconditionally.

9. The Principle of Positive Self-Talk
Most of the activities you will be required to do concerning self-love have to do with your ability to speak to yourself. Remember that you are on this journey for the long haul; no one else will make you love yourself.

You are at the centre of this process and whatever you say or believe about yourself is what will hold sway in your life. You are building positive self-esteem. As such, you will have to reaffirm all the good you see in yourself.

10. The Principle of Peace with Self
Above all, be at peace with yourself. Where there is love, greater peace reigns supreme. If you are always having internal conflict, negative emotions, and a lack of confidence, you will find it difficult to love yourself.

This last principle is so important because there are a lot of people who are unable to love themselves because they don't feel at peace with who they are. Such people will have to get rid of the conflict and settle for a life of peace where love can thrive.

Life can be very dynamic. Some things may happen and spring up on you causing you to lose your peace, but you must be resolute in your determination to love yourself and enjoy peace even as you build higher self-esteem.

These principles will work best when you are deliberate about utilizing them. I always urge readers to look beyond the words on the written page. Instead, readers should think about how these words will come alive through actionable steps.

If you have already practised some of these principles, strengthen your resolve to do more with them. If you haven't worked on any of them yet, be determined to act today. You will be amazed at the extent of growth and improvement you make with your self-esteem.

Finally, we are getting to the very last chapter. I am so excited because it is a culmination of all we have learned from the beginning until now. You already know that this last chapter deals with the concept of sustenance, so let's get right to it.

Chapter Fifteen

The Art of Sustaining Self-Esteem

Well, we are in the last part of our journey, and I believe it has been as rewarding an experience for you as it has been for me. When we started, you had a lot of questions, and as we made progress, you discovered the answers you sought. Good self-esteem is a prerequisite for success in life, and knowing how to build it is a skill that is necessary for growth.

With every good thing that has a beginning, there is also an end. The end of this journey is here, but it is the start of greater things to come, because unlike when we started, you are now equipped with information that will upgrade your life for good.

Self-esteem is not built by just reading a book. Oh, if that was the pathway, by now there would be fewer people with low self-esteem, right? However, a man has got to do more than just read; he must take action, try, fail, and try again until he perfects the process.

So, with all you have read thus far, try not to get it right all at once. It takes time to build solid self-esteem, and if you put in the work, you will reap the rewards of such an effort. This chapter aims to show you ways through which you can SUSTAIN all you have read up to this point.

Let's talk about sustenance for a while, shall we?

When a person learns how to do something, they gain a skill or new ability. If the person exercises that ability for a while, they will become very good at it. But if they are unable to maintain the pace with which to do it repeatedly, they will gradually lose that skill without even knowing it.

Sustainability is about doing something long enough that it becomes a part of you. It is like maintaining a new car; you drive it for a while and then once in a while you take it to the mechanic for regular checks. Now, if you fail to carry out those regular checks, the car will break down someday, and then you will spend more fixing it.

Now you know all about how to build self-esteem and what you must do to make it a vital part of your life. But how do you sustain all you learned now? How can you ensure that the lessons you've gained remain with you for a long time? How do you maintain the standard you've built? The answers to the questions above lie within the steps you can take below.

How to Sustain a Very High Self-Esteem

1. Always Do the Best You Can
One way of sustaining all you have learned is by striving to do your best. With whatever lesson you want to implement, put in the best effort, give your all, and avoid being mediocre.

When you are committed to doing your best, you will enjoy higher self-esteem. There will be a feeling of satisfaction within you knowing that you are on the right path and your efforts will be victorious.

You can be the best all the time!

2. Enjoy Positive Relationships
High self-esteem can be sustained when you nurture positive relationships. You will become a product of the people you hang out with the most. So, if you are always around those who bring down

your self-esteem with hurtful words, it is time to re-evaluate your relationships.

At this point, you are looking at creating new bonds with people who have great personality traits. The more time you spend with great people, the better your chances of improving your self-esteem. Positive relationships are complementary, so ensure that you also add value to the people you spend time with. Give more to get more.

3. Be Happy Every Day

Happiness happens from a place of content satisfaction. For you to sustain your self-esteem goals, you must ensure that you are committed to your happiness.

Every day, wake up with a smile on your face knowing that you can be the happiest human being in the world. As you build self-esteem, you will observe that you are always pleased and content with yourself.
Let happiness lead you to a life of fulfilment and ever-growing self-esteem.

4. Take on the Gratitude Challenge

The gratitude challenge requires you to take account of everything you are grateful for on your journey. This is one very impactful way of sustaining your self-esteem. Look around you right now; there is so much to be thankful for. If you are not conscious of this, you will live a miserable life.

Practise the gratitude challenge every day by counting your blessings and giving your self-esteem the daily boost it requires. One of the ways to implement the gratitude challenge is by keeping a gratitude journal.
Take the journal with you everywhere you go and keep your records. At the end of the day go through all you wrote down and go to bed smiling with a heart full of joy.

5. Cultivate Healthier Habits

We dedicated a chapter to addictions and how they can ruin your self-esteem. Well, for you to sustain all you have learned, you must cultivate the right habits.

Adopt habits that are productively positive, inspiring, and cause you to focus on your goals. Read good books, join a self-esteem men's club, exercise, etc. These are some of the most productive habits you can create.

You will always be a product of the habits you build, so watch closely and pay attention to the things you often do; they will determine how far you go in building your self-esteem.

6. Do What You Love

This step should be taken seriously if you truly want to sustain all you have learned. By doing what you like, you will be positioning yourself as a man who loves himself and is passionate about living on his terms.

Do not allow anyone or any circumstances to force you into doing what you don't like or want. With firmness of heart and a resolution to do only what inspires you, your self-esteem is bound to experience a significant improvement.

Let love lead you on this path; love is the light that never misguides.

7. Forget About Perfectionism

The idea of perfectionism doesn't exist!

No one is perfect; everyone is a work in progress. So don't beat yourself up because you are not perfect. Be inspired to do your best and forget about the idea of being perfect.

There is beauty in trying to be a better person, and when you accept yourself for who you are without the pressures of wanting to be perfect, you will be able to build high self-esteem that is sturdy and inspiring to others.

8. Be Your Own Best Friend

You are all you've got at the end of the day. You have a responsibility to be your own best friend, so play that role well. Learn to advise yourself and cheer yourself on when you win. Also, learn to be your source of strength when the chips are down.

Some people who have experienced low self-esteem often say that they got to that point because no one was there for them when they needed a hand. However, think about it this way; if you were your own best friend, would you rely on someone else for support. Even if you had a perfect support system, you would still be able to handle your issues well by yourself.

9. Avoid Negative Environmental Factors

There are factors in your environment and immediate sphere of contact that conflict with your plans for improved self-esteem. Now is the time to identify those factors and avoid them altogether.

Adverse environmental factors should never be a consideration, especially if you are keen on growing on this journey. Adverse environmental factors may be in the form of neighbours who try to intimidate you with properties they've got.

Whatever type of negativity abounds in your environment, avoid it and protect your mental space from it.

10. Try Something New Often

Who doesn't love new things? Everyone does! So try them; new skills, new books, clothes, friends, experiences etc. People who suffer from low self-esteem always try to shy away from new things because they hold on to their comfort zone.

After reading this book, the only thing you should hold on to is a renewed mindset that aids the changes you want to see in your self-esteem. So be open and free; be willing to take on new adventures because life is all about learning and growing.

If you try something new and you don't like it, you will learn a lesson - but never stop trying!

11. Remember Why You Need Good Self-Esteem
Always remind yourself why you are embarking on this journey. Sometimes you need to be told, so you maintain focus and go ahead with your plans.

When it seems like you are going off course, remind yourself of the values you have and pursue your goals with vigour and focus. It will not always be a pleasant journey, and things will not always go as planned, but one thing is sure in the end, your self-esteem will not remain at the same level.

Consciously and deliberately work on yourself as you aspire to build unshakeable self-esteem.

12. Come Back to the Lessons in This Book
At every turn on this adventure, make sure you come back to the experiences in this book. You shouldn't read through and forget everything you've learned. If you have an issue with any area we have treated in previous chapters, go back to the section to remind yourself of the solutions and steps that were given.

This book is your ultimate guide and best friend; read, read again, and share the lessons with other people. You will be building a network of people that have high self-esteem just like you.

13. Trust Your Decisions

On the path of sustainability, you will be required to make a lot of choices, and it is imperative that you trust the decisions you make. A man who is undecided will be confused - and being confused is a feature of low self-esteem.

If you have trained your mind to recognise and appreciate the best of life, you will always arrive at a favourable conclusion when making decisions. If you don't trust yourself enough, you may have to lean on other people's opinions. And you know what they say about the views of others - they just may not fit with yours.

14. Don't Go Back to Your Shell

Regardless of what happens to you on this journey, never go back to the shell of low self-esteem. Fight off the desire to go back at all costs and maintain the same consistency you've created with your self-esteem.

At some point, you may feel the urge to go back because you are pressured, but if you resist it with great attributes and a renewed mindset to keep up with the journey, you will succeed.

The shell you think you can go back to is not the solution; it is a trap that will take you back to what you should be running from.

15. Create a Pattern

Patterns are like habits - but you can be way more consistent with them. So, with models, you must consider some of the good things you can do that will enhance your self-esteem and be committed to doing them REGULARLY.

With patterns, you can imbibe the right activities and traits all at once. You will also be able to inspire someone else to develop their self-esteem as you share your story.

So, when you wake up at the same time of the day and do the same exciting things that make you happy, you can watch your self-esteem receive a significant boost.

Knowledge isn't power; it is the APPLICATION of knowledge that is power. Knowing what to do doesn't cause any change within you; it is doing it and succeeding at it that transforms your life.

So, with all you have learned now, ensure that you are not only building self-esteem but also sustaining it.

There is one more section you should read; it is the concluding section that ultimately brings the book to an end. There is a special message in that chapter for you, hurry over there now and get started.

Conclusion

What an incredible journey we have had, and it all comes to an end right here. From gaining information on the meaning of self-esteem to learning about self-acceptance and other vital life processes needed to boost your self-esteem.

What we have achieved together with this book will go a long way in helping you build higher self-esteem. It also positions you as an Alpha-male in whatever industry or environment you find yourself. The chapters you read through contain lessons that will be extremely useful to you long term.

So, what is the special message I've got for you in this concluding section? It is a message about the power of being proactive. There are millions of men out there who can relate to everything they have read in this book, yet they lack self-esteem.

The reason for their inability to continue with all they've learned is because they are not proactive enough. In life, we've got two kinds of people; the PROACTIVE and the REACTIVE. The proactive individuals take steps to get what they want, and they succeed.

The reactive ones, on the other hand, wait for situations to happen to them. As such, they end up not being able to achieve anything long term. You should aspire to become a proactive person who can bring the words in this book to life through consistent and sustainable action-plans.

People who lead with great self-esteem are also proactive enough to reach out to others who haven't attained such heights in life. As you help others improve how they feel about themselves, you will be able to solidify all you've gained, as well.

The previous chapter elucidated on the art of sustainability; you were given some steps on how you can sustain all you've learned. From time to time, go back to that chapter and remind yourself what you can do to maintain the self-confidence you've gained.

The book comes to an end here but guess what? It is the start of a brand-new journey for you. Look ahead with faith, give your confidence a significant boost, and don't stop improving on yourself.

I look forward to reading your testimonials as you proactively apply the tips you've been given.

Remember that all good things take time, but with determination and a commitment to excellence, you will stand out from the crowd. Thank you for being such a good sport and sticking it out with me through this book. It is time for you to go forth and win with the most positive attitude towards life and unshakeable self-esteem.

Best wishes to you now and always!!